"Letting go was the hardest thing I've ever done as a leader—and the most liberating. Once I finally stopped micromanaging every corner of my business, everything opened up: more freedom, more creativity, more growth. *Surrender to Lead* nails it. The Results Equation aligns perfectly with *The Let Them Theory*: trust people, create the conditions, and let them rise. That's where real leadership begins."

MEL ROBBINS, *New York Times* bestselling author and host of *The Mel Robbins Podcast*

"*Surrender to Lead* flips the traditional script on leadership—and that's exactly why it's so powerful. With courage and clarity, Jessica and Joe reveal how our obsession with control can hold us back from the very growth we seek. Their personal stories and research make a compelling case for letting go—not of standards or ambition but of the illusion that we can force success. If you're ready to stop gripping tighter and start leading with greater impact, this is the guide you've been waiting for."

DR. MARSHALL GOLDSMITH, Thinkers50 #1 executive coach and *New York Times* bestselling author of *The Earned Life*, *Triggers*, and *What Got You Here Won't Get You There*

"*Surrender to Lead* is truly different from other leadership books. Jessica and Joe have taken a counterintuitive approach to finding what works for leaders and to challenging conventional thinking, and they've laid out a distinct path to getting results and finding new ways to win. 'Surrendering' isn't something to be feared by those in leadership positions; rather, this book makes clear it's what effective leaders do to ensure success for their companies and everyone around them."

BILLY BEANE, senior advisor to the managing partner, Oakland Athletics, and subject of the bestselling book and Oscar-nominated movie *Moneyball*

"*Surrender to Lead* is a wonderful, paradigm-shifting book that challenges the illusion of control and shows how true leadership is found in trust, authenticity, and creating the right conditions for people to thrive. Jessica Kriegel and Joe Terry offer a compelling framework for moving from force to flow in unlocking greater results by focusing on belief, culture, and empowerment. This is a timely and transformative guide for leaders ready to elevate others and achieve outstanding outcomes."

STEPHEN M. R. COVEY, *New York Times* and #1 *Wall Street Journal* bestselling author of *The Speed of Trust* and *Trust & Inspire*

"*Surrender to Lead* is a powerful invitation to rethink what true leadership looks like. Jessica Kriegel and Joe Terry challenge the myth of control and offer a smarter, more human path forward—one rooted in trust, clarity, and purpose. Their message is timely, urgent, and exactly what today's workplace leaders need to hear."

JOHNNY C. TAYLOR JR., SHRM-SCP, president and CEO, Society for Human Resources Management (SHRM), and *Wall Street Journal* bestselling author of *Reset*

"*Surrender to Lead* captures what I've felt my whole career but couldn't name—the paradox that the more you try to control people, the less they give you their best. Jessica Kriegel and Joe Terry show how letting go—trusting your teams and focusing on purpose—unlocks extraordinary results. Every leader who cares about people and performance needs this book."

KELLI VALADE, CEO, Denny's

"*Surrender to Lead* dismantles the illusion of control and invites leaders to embrace humility, trust, and love as catalysts for powerful transformation. With rigor and heart, Jessica Kriegel and Joe Terry propose a courageous redefinition of leadership that puts people first and proves that human-centered cultures are more fulfilling and effective."

HUBERT JOLY, former CEO, Best Buy; senior lecturer, Harvard Business School; and bestselling author of *The Heart of Business*

"The root cause of workplace drama is the belief that we can control everything and everyone. Jessica and Joe expose that myth with honesty and precision—and then give us the tools to lead with presence instead of pressure. This book is a manual for ditching the ego and choosing accountability over anxiety."

CY WAKEMAN, *New York Times* bestselling author and founder of Reality-Based Leadership

"As a pro athlete and mom, I've chased the illusion of control—only to discover that peace and clarity live in the art of getting comfortable with discomfort. *Surrender to Lead* isn't just a book—it's the voice in your head when the road feels longest, the toughest, the hardest, and when the finish line seems impossible. It's a reminder that true strength is forged in discomfort, that courage lives in surrender, and that the unknown isn't something to fear but a place where timeless resilience is born. This is the guide that meets you in your darkest mile . . . and carries you through with power, fortitude, stamina, and endless grit."

MEREDITH KESSLER, 11-time Ironman champion, 23-time Ironman 70.3 champion, and voted greatest American female triathlete

"With everything leaders are up against today, Jessica Kriegel and Joe Terry show us the answer isn't tight control—it's learning to let go. *Surrender to Lead* offers the clarity and trust we need to create conditions where everyone can thrive, which is how leaders build something that truly lasts for themselves and the people counting on them."

JIM MCCANN, founder and chairman, 1-800-Flowers.com

"Trust powers great leadership. As a CEO, trust has always been a cornerstone of my leadership philosophy—the magic glue that holds together personal and professional relationships. *Surrender to Lead* explores why control doesn't scale but trust does. A must-read for leaders ready to embrace this approach to achieve exceptional outcomes."

ARON AIN, executive chair, UKG, and author of *WorkInspired*

"Jessica and Joe have captured my very own early style of leadership and management. For years I was successful because I was brutally organized and would hold people accountable through intimidation and my foolproof system of accountability—because of my own insecurity. Accomplishment and praise from others were my drugs of choice. I got things done but left lots of bodies in my wake. In my mid-30s, I realized my mistaken belief that control was the way and that I needed to change. The last half of my career, I just hired great people, trusted them, and set them up for success. It was hard at first, but I slowly was able to totally let go—then my career and results soared, as well as my marriage. I wish I'd had this book way back when I started out."

LEE COCKERELL, former executive vice president, Walt Disney World® Resort, and author of *Creating Magic*

"What if the gateway to real leadership accountability, enhanced performance, and growth means embracing the opposite of what we've long been taught to believe? That's the intriguing premise of *Surrender to Lead*, a powerful wake-up call for leaders addicted to control. Through courageous storytelling and simple, powerful ideas, Jessica Kriegel and Joe Terry show how surrender isn't weakness but the path to a new set of answers in today's uncertain world. If you want to build a culture where clarity, accountability, and trust replace control, exhaustion, and fear—read this book. But more than that, surrender to it."

JEAN GOMES, *New York Times* bestselling author; founder of Outside Consulting; and Professor of Practice, UCL Global Business School for Health

"Creating a culture of accountability within our agency is not merely an initiative; it is essential to our mission of protecting Georgians. The insights and methodologies we embraced from the *Surrender to Lead* have provided us with the clarity and alignment necessary to begin to transform our agency into a certified great place to work. This collective commitment not only enhances our operational effectiveness but also strengthens our resolve to serve our communities with integrity and excellence."

TYRONE OLIVER, commissioner, Georgia Department of Corrections

"I spent decades learning how to get the best out of my players, and in the era I played, the coach was in control—that was their job. However, real leadership isn't about control—it's about care. Great leaders let go of ego, create connection, and put the team first. My whole philosophy was to hand control over to the team. How do you surrender, and—more importantly—how do you systemize surrender while not abdicating your responsibility as a coach or leader? The result of this counterintuitive approach was our (the Sydney Swans') first Premiership in seventy-two years. In *Surrender to Lead*, Jessica and Joe outline the system for building winning teams."

PAUL ROOS, 2005 Australian Sports Coach of the Year, former AFL superstar, and Australian Hall of Fame member

"If you're tired of white-knuckling your way through leadership, *Surrender to Lead* is your permission slip to breathe. It doesn't preach. It activates growth and momentum, on your terms. This is the kind of book that makes you want to show up differently on Monday—and every day after—ready to win."

PAUL EPSTEIN, former NFL and NBA executive, two-time bestselling author, and founder of WIN MONDAY™

"With a million leadership books in print, the obvious question would be, is there room for another one? The answer is, 'Yes, if it adds value and stands out among the many.' This book does, for four major reasons: 1. It focuses on results. Most leadership books don't. They focus on behavior.; 2. It's based on a tremendous amount of research and, more importantly, practice. It shows what has worked in organizations.; 3. In simple ways, it breaks down the complexities of great leadership into key actions to take. 4. Because culture is probably THE most important issue for organizations, it shows how the leader is essentially a catalyst for making culture work. This book is an indispensable guide for any leader wanting to make a difference in terms that are meaningful to the top executives of the organization."

JACK J. PHILLIPS, PHD, chairman, ROI Institute; former bank president; and author of more than a hundred books

SURRENDER
to
LEAD

The Counterintuitive Approach
to Driving Extraordinary Results

Jessica Kriegel   Joe Terry

amplify

an imprint of Amplify Publishing Group

amplify
an imprint of Amplify Publishing Group

www.amplifypublishinggroup.com

Surrender to Lead: The Counterintuitive Approach to Driving Extraordinary Results

Second printing. This Amplify Publishing edition printed in 2025.

For more information, please contact:
Amplify Publishing, an imprint of Amplify Publishing Group
620 Herndon Parkway, Suite 220
Herndon, VA 20170
info@amplifypublishing.com

Library of Congress Control Number: 2025911756

CPSIA Code: PRFRE1225B

ISBN-13: 979-8-89138-488-0

Printed in Canada

Jessica: *To Papino*

Joe: *To God, Katie, Alexa, Kayla, Jessica, and Aron Ain*

CONTENTS

PART THREE: ACCOUNTABILITY

INTRODUCTION

What do an Ironman athlete and a recovered alcoholic have in common?

We both learned the hard way that control doesn't create success—surrender does.

You, like us, were probably taught that great leaders are always in control. Control your emotions. Control your calendar. Control the metrics. Control the outcome. Even control the team—guide the work, direct the energy, make sure everyone stays on course.

Control was seen as competence. It meant discipline, professionalism, resilience, and strength. We were rewarded for staying composed under pressure, for hitting the numbers, for making things happen.

But eventually we learned the truth: Control has a ceiling.

The more we tightened our grip, the more we stalled the very progress we were trying to create.

We are Jessica Kriegel and Joe Terry. Two leaders. Two wildly different lives. One shared realization: What got us here—control, precision, performance—wasn't enough to take us further. What changed everything was surrender.

Joe Terry—a former NFL player, fifteen-time Ironman competitor, and five-time CEO—knows what it means to push limits. His career has been built on discipline, strategy, and brutal efforts to achieve high-performance leadership. As a young man, he was, in his words, just your average Joe. But a relentless pursuit of potential led him to be anything but average. And yet, what ultimately changed everything for him—what brought him inner peace and external success—wasn't working harder. It was learning when to let go.

Jessica Kriegel—a fiercely independent strategist, skeptic of conventional wisdom, and relentless questioner of authority—knows what it means to fight for control. While Joe built his career on physical endurance and structured leadership, Jessica built hers on intellectual rigor and a deep quest to understand human behavior. A child of divorce, she learned early on that certainty is an illusion. So, she clenched her teeth and became an overachiever, an overthinker determined to prove herself at every turn. Alcohol helped to quiet the racing mind and nonstop need for answers—until it didn't, and something needed to change. The moment things finally clicked was when she reached her bottom. Desperate and in deep psychic pain, she gave up. She surrendered. Sobriety came, serenity followed—and then suddenly, opportunity was everywhere. The phone wouldn't stop ringing.

Throughout this book, you'll hear both of our voices. We'll go back and forth, sharing our experiences and our distinct perspectives—one rooted in discipline, physical endurance, and executive grit, the other in intellectual pursuit, overachievement, and personal awakening. You'll see where we differ, where we align, and how surrender shaped us both in ways control never could.

This is a leadership book, yes. But it's also a book about power, belief, and the paradox of control. We've been sold a lie about leadership—that success comes from gripping harder, from pushing, from managing, from controlling. The more effort that we put in, the better our results will be. Doing more, working harder. Grit! (We both loved psychologist Angela Duckworth's megabestselling book with that title when it came out, by the way.) But our work and research have revealed that an obsession with action can limit success. Not because it leads to burnout, which it can, but because it misses the point entirely and fails to solve the root cause of missed results and frustration. The greatest leaders—the ones who drive real results—aren't the ones who control everyone and everything around them. They're the ones who let go.

We hope to change how you think about leadership. We want to challenge what you thought you knew about getting results. And if you surrender to it, it might change how you lead.

SCAN THE QR CODE BELOW TO DOWNLOAD THE FREE RESOURCES MENTIONED IN THIS BOOK

SURRENDERTOLEAD.COM/RESOURCES

Throughout this book, you'll find references to specific exercises designed to help you apply what you're learning and experience real results.

Scan the QR code to access the downloadable templates and tools that accompany these exercises— practical resources to help you implement the principles in your own leadership journey.

CHAPTER 1

THE POWER
OF SURRENDER

Eight minutes into stoppage time in the 2022 World Cup soccer quarterfinals, Cristiano Ronaldo locked eyes with his teammate and stabbed his finger toward an open space on the pitch, his teeth clenched and his body tense. One last urgent command. One final attempt to seize control before it slipped away for good.

Down by a single goal to Morocco, Ronaldo's Portuguese national team threw everything forward in a desperate push for an equalizer, while the Moroccan bench—in a blur of frantic gestures—implored the referee to end the match. The ball moved in the other direction, out from Ronaldo's reach and away from his control. He sprinted forward, but before he could make his move, the referee's whistle pierced the air.

The game was over.

This wasn't just another World Cup. It had been billed as the final showdown between Ronaldo and Argentina's Lionel Messi— the culmination of a decades-long debate. For years, fans had argued passionately over who was the GOAT (the greatest footballer of all time): Ronaldo, with his staggering career goal count, physical dominance, and relentless drive, or Messi, who was smaller, quieter, and often in Ronaldo's statistical shadow yet unmatched in assists and as a builder of team cohesion. Neither had won a World Cup, and a victory in this tournament would be seen by many as the defining accolade. In the end, they never even got to face each other.

As Ronaldo walked off, shattered, the contrast had never been clearer.

Ronaldo knew, as did the rest of the world watching, that this was likely his last chance at winning a World Cup. This one crowning achievement, the one glaring absence in his decorated career that had always been just out of reach, had slipped away for good. That's what made what happened next so hard to watch.

His gait slowed, his eyes dropped to the ground, his jaw clenched, and he walked—not toward his teammates but straight for the tunnel. When he finally did look up, you could see his lips were pursed tight, as if holding something in—his emotion in that moment, perhaps.

A Moroccan player wrapped his arm around Ronaldo's shoulder and reached out for a handshake. Ronaldo extended his hand and nodded as if on autopilot. For a second, it looked normal, a standard postmatch embrace, but his emotions betrayed him. His body stiffened, caught between two versions of himself—the Ronaldo the world expected to see and the Ronaldo who could no longer hold it together.

For a fleeting second, he was still in control. The handshake, the nod, the composed exterior—it was all instinct, years of conditioning forcing him to maintain the image of a man unfazed.

But beneath that carefully maintained surface, something was breaking. He had spent his entire career mastering control—of his body, of his image, of the game itself. But now, at this moment, he didn't know how to lose control. And he didn't want to.

He pulled away, subtly but firmly freeing himself from the first embrace. But before he could escape entirely, another Moroccan player approached. This time, Ronaldo had to speak. He muttered something—just a few words, but enough to make it clear: *Leave me alone.*

And that's when it happened. The momentary effort of forming words, of acknowledging reality, was enough to crack the thin layer of composure he had left. His voice betrayed him, and if you watch that moment closely, that is when he begins to cry.

He did not look at his teammates. He did not acknowledge the Portuguese fans still watching in stunned silence. He barely seemed to notice when a fan ran into him before getting tackled by a bodyguard. He stayed laser-focused on the dark tunnel ahead of him—his escape from the chaos of the field. When he finally reached the darkness, he fell apart. You can see him let go the second his body is in the shadow of the tunnel.

For two decades, Ronaldo had commanded the field, the cameras, the world's attention. His presence was larger than life, his control absolute—every moment calculated. But now, as he stepped into the tunnel, he wasn't just leaving the pitch; he was leaving his lifelong dream behind. It was the end of an era for Ronaldo. He had clung to the belief that if he just did more, he could force the outcome he wanted. But when the final whistle blew, the weight of that belief came crashing down. The truth was undeniable: Effort alone hadn't been enough. His strategy, the one that had defined his entire career, had reached its limit.

Eight days later, Messi stood on a podium in the center of the same pitch, a triumphant smile illuminating his face, as he lifted the World Cup trophy—his dream finally realized. Today, Messi is the most decorated player in the history of professional soccer, having won six Golden Boots, forty-five team trophies (including twelve Big Five league titles), four UEFA Champions Leagues, two Copa Americas, and—most importantly—one FIFA World Cup.

The contrast with Ronaldo couldn't have been sharper.

For Ronaldo, winning had always been about his personal effort in creating results. "I've never seen anyone better than me. I have always thought that," he once declared. "There's no player more complete than me. I play well with both feet. I'm quick, powerful, good with the head. I score goals. I make assists."[1]

But unlike Ronaldo, Messi's pursuit had never been about personal accolades or chasing the title of the greatest. He didn't win by controlling every detail, dictating every move, or forcing the game to bend to his will. He won by letting go—trusting his team, playing within the flow of the game, and surrendering the need for personal validation.

"It doesn't change anything for me to be the best or not," Messi had said just a year earlier. "And I never tried to be, either." Instead of fixating on proving his superiority, Messi focused on the game itself, on moving the ball, on making his teammates better. "When you look at which sides earn success in football, it is always those who work together as a group, who fight for each other—and every single member holds value and importance."[2]

His career was not built on force but on flow—an unwavering belief that the greatest success isn't something you can force but is something you create with others. And now, with his teammates surrounding him, lifting him on their shoulders, the world could see the truth clearly: Messi's surrender to the team, his belief of the strength of all above any one person, had brought the ultimate reward.

Messi's approach wasn't just philosophical—it showed up in the numbers. He played for the team. Messi had 381 career assists, compared to Ronaldo's 257. He made more key passes, created more scoring chances, and facilitated more goals for those around him. Meanwhile, Ronaldo scored 927 career goals but needed 182 more games than Messi to reach that total. Ronaldo was more dominant individually, but Messi's impact on his team's overall success was greater.

What differentiated these two legendary athletes wasn't just skill—it was their entire approach to success. Messi trusted the game, the team, and the process. Ronaldo fought it. And in the moment that mattered most, that fight consumed him.

Ronaldo was trapped in a faulty belief that if he just controlled his teammates and the flow of the game, he would win. When the final whistle blew, the weight of that belief came crashing down. The game had moved on. Time had moved on. And he was still clinging to air, unable to change what had already slipped away.

Ronaldo was caught in what we call the Action Trap—the all-too-common belief that if you simply push harder, control more, and demand more, you will eventually get the result you want. But as he eventually discovered, the more you try to control everything, and everyone, the more they end up controlling you.

The Action Trap

In business, many leaders become stuck exactly where Ronaldo found himself—exhausted, frustrated, and fixated on control as the solution.

Having a sense of control is undeniably seductive. It feels powerful. It feels productive. It feels like the way things get done. From the moment we take our first steps, we learn that effort creates results. Work hard, study hard, train hard—success is always within reach if we try harder.

The Action Trap is in part so seductive because it works—to an extent. If you push hard enough, demand more, and implement enough new strategies, you will likely see some improvement.

In 2023, we engaged in a research project with a professor at the Stanford Graduate School of Business to measure what drives growth in business. The study analyzed 243 companies, assessing their purpose, their strategy, their culture, and their results. What we found was that companies with bad culture and who were stuck in the Action Trap were able to drive 10.1% growth during the three years of the study. That is nothing to dismiss.

This is also where the Action Trap becomes most dangerous: It creates the perception that control, that teeth-clenching grit, yields strong, lasting results.

But companies that dug deeper—focusing on the underlying drivers of people's actions—and had a strong culture grew by 42.2% in that same period. More than 4X the growth.

Leaders who push harder and force more structure may see short-term improvements, just like Ronaldo's relentless effort made him one of the most dominant goal scorers in history. But over time, control creates ceilings. It caps growth, suffocates innovation, and burns out the very people it depends on. Ronaldo's career was proof of this. He won plenty. But he never won the Big One.

Leaders caught in the Action Trap don't realize they're stuck. To the contrary, it feels like they're doing everything right. They double down on effort, micromanage people and details, demand urgency from their teams, and stack calendars with meetings to "drive alignment." But instead of generating momentum, they create bottlenecks. Instead of inspiring ownership, they breed dependency. Instead of scaling success, they exhaust themselves and their teams. They question why younger generations won't follow their example, baffled when relentless pressure doesn't inspire. The harder they try, the more control slips through their fingers.

The instinct to fall into the Action Trap isn't so deeply rooted just because it works for a while—it's because it taps into something far more fundamental. A primal belief, buried deep in our subconscious: If I can control the world around me, I will be safe.

We don't just seek control for power. We seek it for protection.

I (Jessica) spend most of my workdays doing keynotes at conferences. I have the same routine every time: I walk the halls to see what kind of audience I'll be talking to, I find my way to the ballroom, I do the sound check, and then I find a seat and wait to take the stage.

While I wait, my nerves start to build. It doesn't matter how many speeches I've given—I get nervous every time. I start thinking about all the things that aren't quite right.

The spotlight is too bright. The room is too cold. The confidence monitor is broken. The audience looks like they're not particularly open to hearing a blond chick tell them about leadership. Of course, none of this is in my control. And some of it isn't even true. It is just my perception. In reality, I have one job: to get on stage, give the talk I was hired to give, and go home. But in my head, it would be better if I was running the show. If only the lights were turned down just a little. If only they turned up the thermostat. If only the audience was a little more open-minded. These thoughts are all manifestations of my ego. I am afraid.

We all have that in us. That belief that if things could just be the way we think they should be and if only people would do what we want them to do, everything would be better. Maybe we would be less afraid. And we tell ourselves that we're just trying to make improvements. We're optimizing, or fixing inefficiencies. We're problem-solving, bringing order to the chaos. But other times, we're not being so altruistic. There are also those times we just want things to be better for ourselves, even if it comes at someone else's expense.

As it turns out, intention doesn't matter. Whether we think we're acting for the greater good or purely out of self-interest, the outcome is usually the same: Things eventually don't go our way.

The audience doesn't laugh at my jokes. The project deadline is missed. We didn't get our bookings target for the quarter. The kids are late for school. The dog ate the shoe. Whatever happens, we know it could have been better if it had been different. We double down. We get frustrated and resentful.

But the problem isn't the world. It is our desire for control and the delusion that it can be obtained.

But what is really driving that desire? Fear.

Fear that we'll lose something that we have or fear that we won't get what we need. Fear that if things don't go the way we want, it won't be right. Fear of what others will think. Fear we won't get the recognition we think we deserve.

The irony, of course, is that in our desperate attempt to control everything, we create our own problems. We manufacture stress, resentment, and frustration—all because we're clinging to the belief that we can force reality to bend to our will.

We get so locked into this control mindset that we start believing we are responsible for everything. That if we don't manage it, something will go wrong. We become deluded into thinking we can architect reality itself.

At its core, this isn't about leadership or business or even circumstances—it's about self-centeredness. We see things from our perspective. We want what we want. And when reality doesn't cooperate with what we want, we fight it.

I (Jessica) know exactly where I got the desire for control—and the delusion that I could obtain it by force of will—in my head. When I was eighteen, I joined a cult.

Not the kind with flowing robes, shaved heads, or doomsday predictions, but a subtler breed—one with conference rooms, name tags, and the alluring promise of control over one's destiny.

It was a weekend seminar led by a charismatic businessman who promised limitless success. The message was simple: Your thoughts create your reality.

I remember him saying, "You are the writer, director, and producer of your movie. Your word is law in your universe." And I ate it up.

I left that seminar convinced that I had cracked the code of life. That I could literally bend reality to my will. Fresh from the seminar, I put my new manifestation skills to work. I visualized $10,000 in my bank account. I journaled about the money. I visualized spending it on a trip to Europe. I believed in my ability to make it happen. And then, after taking a summer job selling books door-to-door, I checked my balance one day, and there it was, $14,000.

Across the country, Joe was on an analogous journey—although under a different set of circumstances. He devoured Napoleon Hill's *Think and Grow Rich*, absorbing its lessons on persistence, self-mastery, and the disciplined mind. He wasn't waiting for the universe to deliver; he was building success through mindset and resilience—persistent force of will.

I manifested my way to the C-suite, with a half-million-dollar side hustle as a keynote speaker and a weekly segment on CNN. Joe muscled his way through five CEO gigs with record growth, two exits, fifteen Ironmans, and a stint in the NFL. From the outside, both of us embodied the American Dream, living proof of its promise. We had built our success on the same belief: *Success is a matter of will.*

But what we didn't see—what our culture rarely warns us about—is what happens when that belief is taken too far. We had molded our lives through will and relentless action, but we were in the Action Trap—always running, always pushing, never escaping the snare of doing more. Thinking, actually believing, that this was obtaining results. We mistook the effect for the cause.

When you believe success is purely a matter of will, there is no finish line. No moment of arrival. Because the second you achieve one goal, another one appears, demanding even more effort, even more control, even more will.

I made $14,000 selling books. Could I double it?

Joe finished another Ironman. Could he beat his time?

I built a side hustle. Could I turn it into a full-time empire?

Joe led the company to $100 million in revenue. Can he get us to $200 million?

The more we achieved, the more we believed that action was the answer to everything. Not just *any* action—our action. The expression and assertion of our selves. Our personal and singular knowledge or ability could create better results through sheer force of effort. And yet, for all our striving, we were never done. Instead of feeling fulfilled, we were trapped in a cycle of perpetual doing—convinced that if we just worked harder, pushed further, and controlled more, we would finally get there.

But where was *there*? And why were we so desperate to reach it?

Fear-Based Beliefs Limit Results

These anecdotes aren't just convenient illustrations of a point distinct to us. Rather, they express an approach embedded in business culture. In today's corporate culture, fear-driven self-will has become a dysfunction. We reward action, performance, and attempts to exercise control at work, even when it compromises or shortchanges results.

Fear breeds rigidity. Fear propels people forward, into the Action Trap.

When people feel unsafe, they don't experiment, they don't challenge assumptions, and they certainly don't take the kind of risks that lead to meaningful change. Instead, they cling to what is known, what is predictable, what won't get them singled out.

Leaders, meanwhile, mistake compliance for alignment. They assume that because no one is vocally resisting, people are taking accountability for driving results. But the reality is that just because resistance isn't voiced, it doesn't mean it doesn't exist. It's often just being buried. Not because people don't see the problems, but because they want to be liked. They know the leader ultimately decides who stays and who goes.

Your ego is at the root of it all. Fear of losing control. Fear of being wrong. Fear of exposing vulnerability.

And so, we shove it down. We silence uncertainty. We convince ourselves that keeping the machine running—obtaining results through the exercise of personal willpower—is what works. But fear doesn't disappear—it festers.

Then, someone is given an accolade on a team call for working on the weekend, and we have an experience that leads to a new belief: *Working harder will get me rewarded. I should work harder.*

And just like that, we're trapped in a downward spiral.

The more we fear, the harder we work. The harder we work, the more disconnected we become. The more disconnected we become, the more fragile we feel. So we cling even tighter to the very structures that got us here in the first place. For some of us, it becomes too much.

My (Jessica's) father was the CEO of a color separation and printing business called Power Color for fifteen years. Business was good for a decade, although the growth was slow. But when the Macintosh came out, Power Color began to struggle. His business was being cannibalized by college kids on their new computers. He tried everything to save it. He pulled all-nighters for three nights in a row once a quarter when he was on deadline. He made his team come in on weekends.

As the fear of losing his business grew, he developed anxiety and depression. He became curt with his colleagues, and some left. He didn't bring in enough revenue one quarter, so he stopped paying taxes and skipped a few rent payments. The struggle to control the outcome got him nowhere and sank him deeper into despair. The company was completely dysfunctional, unable to adapt to the changing technology, and before he knew it, he closed the doors.

Fear, in short, is the driving force behind every dysfunctional dynamic we see in business, from departmental silos to quiet quitting to complete failure. It pushes us to clamp down in a desperate bid to protect what we have. It ensnares us in the Action Trap—the more we struggle, the tighter the bind. Fear-based control only breeds more fear. It creates secrecy, mistrust, and disengagement. And it drags results down.

Fear Creates Organizational Dysfunction

This isn't just an individual problem. It lies within the teams and organizations as well.

The number one issue our clients bring to us—over and over again—is departmental silos. Departments that fail to communicate. Teams that hoard information. Colleagues in conflict over who is to blame for missed targets or who gets credit for made targets.

These companies have value statements around collaboration and shared ownership, but despite the language of unity and teamwork, we are all operating inside a corporate structure that feeds competition, not collaboration.

Workplaces are built like pyramids—wider at the base, narrow at the top. The higher you climb, the fewer seats there are. The corporate ladder isn't built for everyone to succeed; it's built for a select few to make it to the top while the rest are left vying for position. In the world we've built for ourselves, success isn't just about rising, it is about rising above. Above the competition, above each other, above our peers, above the people who might take our place if we ever slow down.

The experience of working in the corporate hierarchy shapes a belief that success is not just about achieving but about achieving more than the person in the cubicle next to yours. For me to win, you must lose. There's only one VP position open, and three senior directors are vying for the job. Kumbaya.

Information becomes power. Knowledge is leveraged. Helping others carries risk—even subconsciously. If opportunities are scarce, visibility becomes currency, and individual contribution is prioritized over shared success. The result is a culture where teamwork is encouraged by leaders but constrained in practice. Silos form not because people refuse to collaborate, but because the system creates conflicting incentives.

People aren't the only ones creating experiences. Processes and structures do too. The result is dysfunction.

We worked with a software company that was experiencing growth but struggling to hit its ambitious targets. Leadership sensed that "what got us here won't get us there" and believed the key to unlocking their next level of success was collaboration.

The sales team was organized around products. Each rep had deep expertise in their product and focused on selling that one product. Leadership encouraged lead-sharing. If a client bought one of our products, they were more likely to buy another. This called for more cross-selling, more communication, and more visibility into each other's pipeline. But despite all the messaging from management, nothing changed.

To fix this, the leader of the sales team planned the entire sales kickoff meeting around solving this problem. For three days in Las Vegas, they did training around cross-selling, shared strategy around the product road map, and—of course—did team-building exercises. They took Myers-Briggs tests, talked about their personalities in breakout sessions, and then bonded over drinks after 5:00. But when the teams returned to work the following week, collaboration remained just as stagnant. They slipped back into the Action Trap.

Frustrated, they came to us—hoping another, better retreat might be the answer. Instead of jumping into action, we asked a simple question: *What beliefs does the team hold that are preventing them from cross-selling?*

As we worked with the teams, a clear pattern emerged. Despite all the rah-rah messaging about teamwork, the system itself was telling a different story. Sales reps were ranked from highest to lowest on a public leaderboard. A Salesforce dashboard tracked individual performance in real time. Quarterly awards celebrated top sellers. The President's Club vacation trip was reserved for the top 10% of the sales reps.

These experiences shaped a belief: If I share my leads, I'm giving my teammate a way to beat me.

Collaboration wasn't failing because people didn't want to work together. It was failing because the system made them compete. No amount of team-building exercises could override the reality that their success was measured individually. Until that changed, no pep talks from the leader would make a difference.

The problem wasn't effort—it was experience. If they wanted new results, they had to create new experiences that shaped different beliefs.

So, they rewired the system.

The leaderboard came down. No more public rankings that pitted reps against each other. Instead, they introduced team-based dashboards that tracked collective wins—how many customers expanded their purchases, how much additional value they unlocked together.

The compensation plan evolved. Individual quotas still mattered, but hitting them unlocked eligibility for team-based incentives. The coveted President's Club trip? No longer reserved for the top 10% of lone wolves. Once targets were achieved, teams could now qualify together.

The sales meetings also changed. Instead of celebrating solo wins, they showcased collaborative deals—where reps worked across product lines to land bigger, better contracts.

The leaders focused on creating new experiences, and the beliefs shifted. Reps who once guarded their leads started proactively connecting teammates with clients. Conversations changed. Pipeline visibility improved. Cross-selling surged. And in the end, the company shattered its revenue targets—not because leadership kept saying "collaborate"—but because they made collaboration the way to win.

This company experienced a common roadblock to growth. Corporate structure often rewards competition while promoting the language of unity, leaving individuals navigating an unspoken truth: When resources, promotions, and recognition are limited, the instinct for self-preservation—driven by fear—takes over.

This isn't a failure of character. It's a response to the environment—a rational adaptation to a predisposition that is ingrained in us and in a system designed to create winners and losers. And nowhere is this more evident than in the way *layoffs* have become an accepted, even expected, part of corporate life.

The experience of witnessing or enduring layoffs reinforces a painful belief: Security is an illusion.

One quarter, a company celebrates record earnings; the next, entire teams are cut in the name of efficiency. Years of dedication, long hours, and exceeding expectations offer no real protection. That belief drives action. Self-preservation becomes the priority.

And what happens when self-preservation takes over? People stop giving a shit about shared goals. Call it burnout. Call it disengagement. Call it quiet quitting. But what we're really seeing is a workforce shutting down.

When people feel powerless—when they've given everything to a system that only demands more—they don't rebel. They disconnect. Not out of laziness but out of self-protection. Apathy is the only form of control they have left.

Apathy is a slow death for any organization. It is far worse than rebellion. At least when your employees unionize, they're talking to you. The real threat to business is employee indifference. And yet, instead of recognizing this, leaders keep reaching for more control. They do things like forcing people back into the office to "save our culture." They remain in the Action Trap.

The underlying issue is the belief system that your employees hold. They may fill out your engagement survey, but they know they are still operating within the same system—one where leaders make me commute to work against my will because they think I lack integrity and am slacking off. One where decisions about promotions, raises, and even job security are made by those at the top. This experience shapes another belief: *Disagreeing with leadership—especially publicly—is dangerous and can backfire.*

Challenging a bad idea, offering dissent, or pushing back on a directive isn't just a matter of principle—it's a calculation. Will speaking up put my job at risk? Will it make me seem difficult?

That belief drives silence. People see flaws in strategies but don't say anything. They anticipate problems but let them unfold. They withhold feedback that could change the course of your team, department, or company because of fear. You can change that.

The antidote isn't another round of micromanagement or top-down directives. It's a whole different way of seeing and leading—one that lets us break free from the fear-driven cycle once and for all. This is where we shift to surrender and discover how releasing the delusion of control can transform our teams, our organizations, and ourselves.

The Delusion of Control

Control is a misguided belief. It is a fear-based way of thinking that creates dysfunction and limits growth. This book is about shifting from control to surrender, not as a sign of weakness but as a strategy for leadership and growth.

This is a critical point—surrender isn't about giving up. It's not weakness or passivity. It's about letting go of the delusion of control. You may be confused about what you can and cannot control because we've bought into the story of corporate power.

In the business world, we've all bought into the delusion that those at the top have power. It's the foundational principle of the way things work. Your title includes the word manager, or director, or president, or chief. You have people reporting to you. You have goals that you are accountable for. You tell people what to do. You decide who stays and who goes. You are at the top of the corporate food chain.

But strip away the titles, the org charts, the P&Ls, and what's left? A collection of human beings navigating life the best they can before time runs out. Elon Musk puts his pants on one leg at a time, just like you.

Control is a mirage. That is the paradox of leadership in organizations. The strongest leaders aren't the ones who hold on the hardest. They're the ones who surrender to what they cannot control, focus on what they can, and trust in the process that unfolds.

We surrendered. Not by choice but, like many other leaders caught in the Action Trap, by force.

At separate times, in separate circumstances, we each had a personal moment of clarity—the instant we knew the fight was over. Our proverbial tunnel walk. Jessica was fighting her demons. Joe was fighting his attachment to past performance. We were both caught in the Action Trap. One of us had nothing left to lose. The other had everything to protect.

I (Jessica) was at the end of my rope—burned out, exhausted, and numb. I had spent years trying to control everything: my career, my reputation, my success, my relationships. If I just worked harder, learned more, strategized better, pushed through the exhaustion, I would get where I wanted to go. That was the illusion I lived under.

And then I fell apart—trapped inward and unable to get where

I was supposed to be. Shattered.

It wasn't one dramatic moment—it was a slow collapse, like a bridge eaten away by rust until it crumbles under its own weight. Drinking became routine, the anxiety unmanageable, and the confusion unbearable. I was torching the relationships in my life while always trying to figure out the next move. I had nothing left to give, but I kept forcing myself forward.

One night I was lying on the ground of my bedroom crying and thinking about how much I hated myself when something cracked. Finally, I surrendered. I can't explain it. It felt like a spiritual experience. A thought just came into my head that didn't seem like it was mine, and I gave up. Not in defeat but in acceptance. Acceptance that I wasn't in control—that my relentless grip on everything was the very thing suffocating me. I didn't have all the answers. I couldn't force my way to peace, to a place of serenity. And for the first time, I allowed something bigger than myself to take the lead. That was the first day of my sobriety and a new way of living.

Joe's inflection point looked quite different.

From the outside, he was unstoppable—the Ironman CEO, former NFL player, a relentless competitor, a family man with two wonderful children and a wife of thirty-one years. He was a leader who thrived in the world of resilience and discipline. He ran the company like he trained for races: all-in, all the time. His schedule was punishing, his expectations unrelenting, and his commitment unwavering. He was a private-equity company's dream of a CEO. He was even inducted into his private-equity partner's Hall of Fame for driving results.

And then, his bike crank broke in the middle of a half-Ironman (a story we'll tell in more detail in the next chapter).

That was the first day of a new way of living for Joe. He stopped micromanaging. He traveled less. He trusted his team in ways he never had before. He made small shifts: Instead of telling his managing partners how to structure deals, he asked them how they wanted to structure them. He surrendered—not to failure but to a new way of leading.

I was at my bottom, and he was at the "top," but we both were caught in the Action Trap and forced to surrender just the same. Surrender, it turned out, was the only way out.

The result? For Jessica—it was gig after gig, serenity, and success by any definition. For Joe, it was much the same. His company had its best performance of its thirty-five-year history. That same year, he had his personal best Ironman time (in his fifteenth Ironman, at the age of fifty-nine).

Letting go didn't mean losing control—it meant unlocking something greater than control ever could.

When we realized that, we didn't lose power—we finally stepped into it. This wasn't just personal growth. It was a leadership revelation. And it inspired for us a new definition of surrender and the creation of a new type of leader—the Surrendered Leader:

To surrender is to make a conscious shift from force to flow. It is accepting that you cannot control outcomes, circumstances, teams, not even your direct reports. Surrendered leadership is a strategic letting go of things outside of your control, so that you can fully leverage what you actually do control: yourself.

As a leader, however, your role is not just about yourself. You are operating within the context of others. So, if you are not controlling people or outcomes, then what are you doing as a leader? You are making the personal choice to focus on what you can control while setting up the conditions for others to succeed and thrive.

The Surrendered Leader does not manage actions; they focus on creating the right conditions that drive those actions. You can't force results, but you can create the environment where the right outcomes happen naturally. Your role as a leader is to set the conditions that allow people and organizations to reach their full potential.

What are those conditions called? Culture.

What Is Culture?

So much gets in the way of understanding what culture really is and what its role is in achieving results. In today's age, many see workplace culture as synonymous with, at worst, Ping-Pong tables and pizza parties and, at best, generational dynamics and employee well-being. But leaders are stuck in the Action Trap of culture creation. It can't be fixed with pizza parties or a lecture about bringing your authentic self to work.

Culture is not a vibe. It is the lived experiences of a group unfolding into shared cultural beliefs that create motivation to act and therefore drive results.

This is the premise of what we call the Results Pyramid, and it is the basis of all the work we have done to help businesses like Southwestern Airlines, Ford, Spanx, and Hilton to achieve breakthrough results.[3]

Experiences > Beliefs > Actions > Results

Every action gets a result. It may not be the result you want, but regardless, actions lead to results. This is where most leaders stop. They know what actions they believe will lead to the right results, and so they focus on action. The sales leader checks in with his or her rep and asks about action.

- How many calls did you make?
- How did the sales call go?
- Did you track the call in Salesforce?
- Who are you going to call next?
- Did you have the AI tool listen to your call to give you suggestions on how to improve the call?
- Have you read the book *The Challenger*?

This approach works, to an extent. Recall, the Action Trap is seductive. But ask yourself—what is the lived experience of the sales rep in this scenario? They probably feel irritated and micromanaged. They feel infantilized and nagged. This experience leads them to a belief: "My manager doesn't trust me," or "My manager only cares about the numbers, not me." That belief shapes their mindset and therefore their action. Maybe they start doing the bare minimum to avoid scrutiny. Maybe they get defensive. Maybe they quiet quit. Maybe they get stressed out and the stress lowers their confidence, which affects their performance.

And yet, the manager is confused. "Why aren't they taking accountability?" "Why aren't they meeting their quota?" The Results Pyramid goes both ways. The employee is now creating an experience for the manager. The manager develops a new belief: This is a bad sales rep. And they take new action: It's time to move on. That leads to a result—six months of training a new hire and the process continues to unfold with little change.

Or maybe it's even worse. Maybe this experience reinforces a preexisting belief (thought) that the manager had that "Young people today just don't want to work." This leads to new action, stereotyping generations entirely or avoiding hiring college graduates. In a meeting he says something like, "Young people today are so entitled," and a young person on the Zoom has an experience that leads them to the belief, "My manager sees me as a walking stereotype. He doesn't get me." This leads to an action. And so, you see, the cycle continues.

This is culture. Put simply:

Culture is how people think and act to get results.

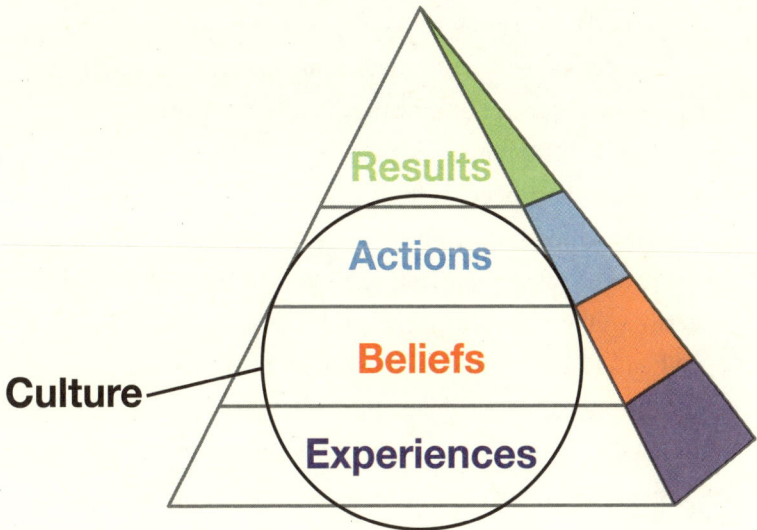

From Control to Culture:
What Are We Surrendering To?

The real work of leadership is not in managing actions but in creating the right experiences that shape the beliefs (or the culture) in which the right actions happen, and results follow.

That requires surrender. But what exactly are we surrendering to?

We are surrendering to the natural unfolding of beliefs and actions that emerge from changed experiences that result from meaningful contact between people and structures that influence and change beliefs—ultimately yielding results. Instead of forcing results through rigid structures and relentless effort, the Surrendered Leader focuses on transforming experiences to shift beliefs. Once beliefs change, actions evolve organically, leading to the desired outcomes with less friction.

Surrender happens not by giving up on action or results but by letting go of control of how they manifest—trusting that the right actions will follow once people think differently. You are surrendering your need to impose your will and your way on the people you work with, and you are setting the conditions for explosive results that come from the empowerment of everyone's collective will on the team . . . not just yours.

When a leader creates an experience of trust, autonomy, and genuine support, the rep develops a belief that they are capable, valued, and empowered. And when they believe that? They take ownership. They innovate. They feel energized and fulfilled. They become accountable.

Instead of focusing purely on actions, great leaders ask:

- What belief do I want my team to hold about me as a leader?
- What belief do I want them to hold about themselves and this company?
- What experience am I creating for my team?
- What experiences are our processes creating for them?

When you get out of the Action Trap, you focus on what you can control, the experiences you create that shape their beliefs. Rather than just tracking calls and micromanaging activity, imagine if the leader in the scenario above took a different approach:

- What did you learn from that sales call?
- What felt like a win?
- What's one thing you'd do differently next time?
- How can I support you in getting better?
- Are you feeling fulfilled in this role?

This shifts the conversation from accountability through control to accountability through belief-shifting. The rep walks away with a different experience—one that tells them "My leader believes in me." That belief turns into new action and ultimately better results.

This is the difference between managing actions and shifting beliefs.

The Results Pyramid offers a road map for getting out of the Action Trap. If you are only focused on actions and results, then you stay trapped in a cycle of effort and diminishing returns. The deeper work is in shifting the beliefs that drive behavior, because when beliefs shift, actions shift, and your results transform. Forcing your will on the team is not effective. You cannot mandate culture.

Take diversity, equity, and inclusion (DEI), for example. After the firestorm over the death of George Floyd in 2020, companies rushed to mandate DEI with new hires, new programs, and new metrics. But you can't mandate a belief in diversity, in equity, or in inclusion. As DEI became politically unpopular in 2024, it was quickly ripped out of organizations countrywide. But if DEI could be ripped out that quickly, it was never part of your culture in the first place. Companies that had Action-Trapped DEI got the results to match.

As a leader, you have a role in setting the conditions to create results. This involves three key steps:

1. **Clarity**—Create experiences that allow everyone to attain clarity on the purpose, the strategy, and the results you're trying to achieve.
2. **Alignment**—Create experiences that will encourage beliefs to emerge that align with the results you're trying to achieve.
3. **Accountability**—Create experiences that foster a culture of accountability. You can't impose accountability on others, but you can speak the language of accountability and demonstrate it through your own actions, setting the standard for commitment and follow-through.

You'll notice that in all of this work, the only thing you can control is the experiences you create for other people. That's a critical point. These experiences will shift the beliefs of those around you, and those beliefs will lead to action, which will get results. This is how you surrender to lead.

In the coming chapters, we will break this down step by step. The first chapters will explore the surrender shift—why it feels counterintuitive in leadership yet is the key to creating adaptable organizations. Then we explore the role that leaders have in setting the conditions for organizations to drive results. Part 1 will dive into a leader's first task—to create clarity around your purpose, strategy, and culture to get results. This is the Results Equation:

Purpose + Strategy + Culture = Results

Part 2 will explore how to drive alignment around your Results Equation at scale—in particular, how you shift the beliefs of your team so they can adapt to change and drive explosive growth. Finally, part 3 will dig into accountability, the holy grail of results.

Our goal is to create an experience for you through storytelling—one that shifts your belief about leadership. Then you may surrender to lead. We believe that if you do, what you can accomplish is beyond our wildest imagination.

After all, true greatness isn't about controlling every play. It's about elevating those around you. Just ask the GOAT—Messi.

CHAPTER 2

SHIFT TO SURRENDER

The word *surrender* has a negative connotation, especially for winners. We've been trained to associate surrendering with quitting or admitting defeat. But it's not a white flag. It is quite the opposite.

Surrender is an understanding of the current reality and a letting go of the desire for control—taking ultimate accountability for the current situation. It is not an abandonment of effort. It is not easy, and usually surrender includes struggle. Just like in nature, where salmon swim upstream to spawn, surrender requires effort. It's not about passivity. It's about embracing what is necessary (relative to the way that things are) and encountering that fact in an authentic way.

I (Joe) remember the Oregon sky that morning—crisp and almost electric with the promise of a good race. My training leading up to the race was on point. After a very fast (downstream) swim, I was off on my bike, pushing my body to its limits. I was having a great day. Then it happened. I was cruising around mile forty-five of the fifty-six-mile bike leg. My heart was thrumming with the steady confidence I had earned from years of training. I was dialed in.

Then came the shift.

Suddenly, a violent jolt under my right foot. My mind reeled—maybe just a loose pedal? But with each rotation, the problem escalated. It wasn't just a rattle; the crank was peeling off the bike. *Oh shit*, I thought. This thing is going to break, and for the first time ever, I am not going to finish a race I started. I have eleven miles left in the bike leg, but I'm not going to make it. I have been in over a hundred races and have finished every single one. No matter the weather, no matter how tired, no matter the obstacle, I promised myself I would never give up—I would finish. But this was different. This was out of my control.

I started running through my story in my head. How would this look? How would I tell people what happened? Yes, I quit, but everyone would understand. My bike broke. What else could I do? No one could blame me for a mechanical issue. The panic started to rise in my chest. I could feel my body tensing, bracing for the heartbreak of dropping out.

Then I remembered my eighty-nine-year-old father waiting for me at the finish line. He had never seen me quit. How many more races would he be there for, to watch me cross the finish line? There were a few seconds of back-and-forth in my head and then, finally, I stopped fighting.

Not the race; I stopped fighting reality.

I had a moment of surrender when I realized that no amount of raw will could unbreak a crank. And no amount of justification could erase the truth: The crank was shot, but my leg still worked. In that moment I put all my faith into three things: what I could control, the training I'd done, and my purpose in that moment—my father at the finish line.

I stopped overthinking, and I zeroed in on what I still had.

I clipped in my left foot, let the right crank dangle, and said out loud, "Fuck it." I pedaled the rest of the race with one leg. My speed plummeted from more than twenty-two miles per hour to eleven miles per hour. All my competitors that I had been passing earlier in the race happily started passing me. But my mind wasn't bothered by them. I had shifted from "What if?" to "What now?" Full surrender to accountability for my current circumstance. And I pressed on—not out of stubbornness but out of calm conviction that, broken crank be damned, this was how I'd finish the race. I was responsible for the effort; God was responsible for the outcome.

From the outside, I know it might have looked like sheer will-power, the kind of grit we celebrate when someone refuses to quit. People lined all along the bike course were cheering me on; we all love the story! We call it "pushing harder," or "manifesting success," or "mental toughness." But this wasn't that. I've done that. In fact, I think I've used that tool in my toolbox in almost every race I've ever competed in. But on this day, what propelled me forward wasn't a battle against the bike or the other racers—it was actually letting go of the battle altogether. This is the surrender shift.

When I finally reached the bike finish, I was a sight. My leg was burning. My right crank was dangling uselessly. Spectators gawked at me awkwardly, but I just stayed focused on the next right thing. I finagled my way out of the pedals and switched into my running gear for the half-marathon. The bike was over. Nothing I could do about it now. The pressure had lifted. Instead of carrying the weight of expectation, I was simply in the moment, focused on moving forward towards my dad. I said, "OK let's see what you can do on this run!"

When I crossed the finish line, it turned out to be my best run time I'd had in five years. I found my dad wearing a wide,

glowing smile of pride and gave him a big hug. In that moment I felt something different—I felt lighter. Not because I had pushed through, but because I had let go. The clock didn't just mark my best run; it marked a shift. A lesson that strength doesn't always come from holding on. It can also come from surrender.

This story illustrates a journey that led to a dramatic moment. That journey and moment are relevant, indeed critical, for both individuals and aggregations of individuals into broader organizations. The journey is available to leaders and those they lead.

We call this process the Surrender SHIFT.

1. **S—Stop Fighting Reality**

   Let go of what isn't yours. We exhaust ourselves fighting circumstances and people we can't change. When you stop gripping everything, you're freed to focus on reality, the way it is.

   I stopped fighting reality. "The right crank is broken, but my left leg still works."

2. **H—Have Faith**

   Trust what's unfolding. Remember, surrender for us isn't waving a white flag; it's choosing to believe that there's something more powerful than your own force of will. Maybe it's your team's collective ingenuity, or a higher purpose, or destiny. Faith replaces frantic control with calm confidence. If you're not sure what to have faith in, ask yourself: What do you believe is the source of all good? Have faith in that.

   I had faith in my training and my purpose—to see my dad at the finish line.

3. **I—Identify What's Yours**

   Own what you can control; release what you can't.
   Surrender begins by channeling your energy to what is truly
   within your power: your own choices, beliefs, and actions.
   *I did what I could control. I pedaled eleven miles
   with one leg.*

4. **F—Free Yourself from Fear**

   Fear comes from the preoccupation with the self. Being
   stuck in thoughts about what might happen in the future.
   Move from thinking about yourself to thinking about
   others. Release yourself from your preoccupation with
   how others are thinking of you. Take a few deep breaths
   and fill your heart with love.
   *I freed myself from the fear of losing, of not finishing, of
   looking ridiculous. I replaced the thoughts in my head about
   not finishing with thoughts about my dad.*

5. **T—Take the Next Right Action**

   Move with purpose, not force. Surrender frees you to act
   decisively on what matters most without being enslaved
   by the outcome. Ask yourself, what is the next right action
   that I can take? Even if it's hard, even if there is an easier
   way, what is the next right action?
   I just ran.

When you apply these steps, you shift from a fear-based,
control-centric, self-centered mindset—one that is constantly
pushing further and further into the Action Trap—to one that
embodies surrender.

* * *

Just like Joe, my (Jessica's) own moment of surrender hit when something in my life broke down. But it wasn't a crank. It was my marriage. A few years after my father closed his business, he found his own way to surrender. He bought a motorcycle with a sidecar and took off for a twelve-year trip around the world. I missed him deeply, but when I got pregnant at the age of thirty-three, he decided to come home for good. We were thrilled to have him back. Every morning, we would walk on the river and talk about my baby, whom he nicknamed Violeta until I picked her real name (it's Eleanor). Those morning walks were pure joy—until he died suddenly of a heart attack just months after Ellie was born. I sank into a deep depression, and my alcoholism intensified.

After a year of avoiding my grief and fighting reality, I hit bottom the morning my husband and I ended our relationship. He left the house, and I stood in the silence, stunned by how empty everything felt—inside and out. I didn't know what to do, but I knew I had to *do something*. I wanted to go to the gym, but the car wouldn't start. Then I tried to ride my bike, but the bike had a flat. Then I tried my husband's bike, and the seat was falling off (I guess my story did have a broken bike after all). I was so frustrated. I didn't believe in God at the time. If I had I might have interpreted all these roadblocks as a sign not to go, but I was just angry that things weren't going my way. Finally, I decided to go out for a walk—the same walk I'd been avoiding since my father died because the memory was too painful.

I called my best friend and told him what happened. He asked, "What are you feeling?" and I said I just missed my dad. "What would your dad say?" he asked. I told him my dad wouldn't say anything—he would just do something that made me feel that everything was going to be okay. At that exact second, I looked down and saw brand-new graffiti on the pavement that had never been there before. It spelled out "Violeta." I fell to my knees, sobbing, and said out loud, "I will never question if there is a God again." That was the moment I surrendered. I went through the SHIFT: I stopped fighting, had faith for the first time, owned my responsibility (I was a drunk), freed myself from the fear of grief and sobriety, and took the next right action. I quit drinking.

In writing this book, we realized something that gave me chills. The path I was walking when I saw "Violeta" on the ground—the moment I surrendered for the first time—was the same course where Joe had his best Ironman finish shortly after his moment of surrender. Same location. Different days. But somehow, we both had our most transformational moments on the same stretch of road. It felt like a quiet confirmation that this message, this book, was meant to be.

That profound turning point reverberated through my entire life, compelling me to choose a new way of life. But my commitment to surrender was put to the test only a few months later when I started a new role as chief human resource officer (CHRO) at a tech start-up. In my first executive retreat, we started with a board meeting. Disappointed by the company's performance, the investors demanded drastic cuts—so layoffs became the main topic of the retreat. Like many tech companies, we'd leased pricey Class A office space in 2019 and overhired before COVID-19.

Planning for layoffs occurs behind closed doors, of course. Decision-makers compile lists, work with managers to decide who stays and who goes, juggle spreadsheet targets, then stage-manage the messaging to the team, the public, and stakeholders. That's the

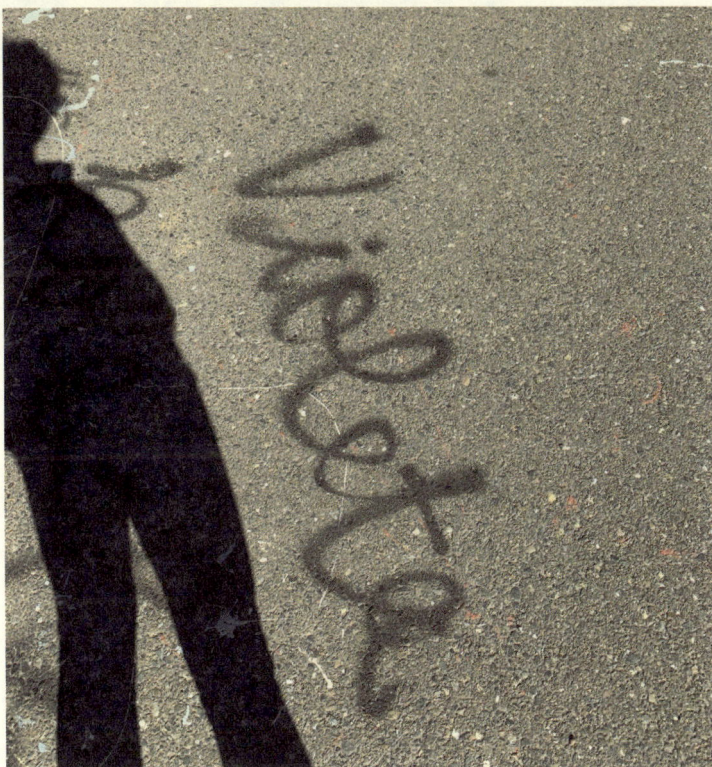

"control" approach—forcing your will on the organization to get what you want. But it doesn't work. Why? Because it's just another iteration of the Action Trap and creates a negative experience for everyone involved. Those who remain feel insecure, and those who leave see every prior gesture of trust as hollow. People conclude that the business doesn't really care about them.

As described earlier, I had just gone through a life-altering experience. I was four months sober and in the midst of a personal transformation. Pain and humility had taught me that my way wasn't working, that control was an illusion, and that the only way forward was to surrender, in alignment with a higher power—honesty, integrity, truth, and doing the next right thing, even when it's hard.

I couldn't bring myself to handle this layoff the traditional way. I'd spent too much of my life dodging the truth and warping reality to fit my own narrative, and it had nearly destroyed me. Now, I was committed to leading using a different path. I chose to surrender at work and in the way I lead.

I decided to **stop fighting reality (S)**. Layoffs were inevitable. There was nothing that could be done about that. But I also could let go of the notion that I had to hide or manipulate the truth. I let go of the old belief that secrecy was the only way to keep the company stable.

Then I **had faith (H)**—faith in my team's maturity and my own values. I chose to trust that everything would happen the way it was meant to and that God was in charge. God is where I place my faith, although it isn't where you have to place yours.

Then I **identified what was mine (I)**: I owned my responsibility as the leader of the team, and I chose to treat people like adults. I owned my decision to open the lines of communication, even if it was uncomfortable. I told the CEO that I believed it was best to tell the team about the upcoming layoffs. This would create the best experience for both the employees who were impacted and those who were retained. He was hesitant but agreed. I set up a Zoom call and told everyone in the HR department that we were having layoffs, that HR was not exempt from the layoffs, and that the months ahead would involve figuring out how many, who, and when. I openly acknowledged the uncertainty ahead. I was transparent and answered their questions. I told them that they might be out of a job soon. And they might not.

It felt risky. My ego was whispering: *What if they panic? What if my top performers leave? What if they all leave?*

I had to **free myself from fear (F)**, reminding myself that if we lost good people, I could still handle the fallout. My integrity was more important than my convenience. I turned my focus from myself to others. I asked for guidance on handling whatever comes next, and I reminded myself that those were all questions about the future anyway. They weren't happening now. And these people deserved to know what was happening.

In short, I **took the next right action (T)** by telling the truth, trusting the process, and continuing to support my team. Surprisingly, my honesty didn't spark panic—it fostered trust. Sure, there was some fear, but I didn't think it was my job to micro-manage their feelings. I thought it was my job to surrender to the business circumstances, to my larger sense of doing the right thing, and to reality.

What happened? Some people started looking for a new job, and some people found them and took them. Others stayed. By the time I had to decide who to lay off, there was no decision to make. The company had right-sized itself to meet the needs of the budget. Those who wanted to stay stayed, and those who wanted to leave left. And both those who stayed and those who left were deeply grateful for the transparency. Contrary to conventional leadership wisdom, surrendering control created stronger bonds, deeper loyalty, and ultimately better results.

In the end, morale actually improved among those who stayed, because the conversation was real. The fear-based, hush-hush approach, the secrecy, the illusions—it all gave way to a love-based approach.

By practicing these steps in the face of every challenge—broken cranks, corporate layoffs, project setbacks, or even your child's missed homework—you gradually retrain your mind to reject fear and choose surrender. You learn to recognize the ego's illusions of separation and scarcity for what they are: false constraints that keep you small and anxious.

When you surrender the need to control everything, you unleash a new kind of power. It's the power to see things clearly, to trust your team, and to act decisively on what actually matters. Over time, this approach builds cultures of real fulfillment and real results.

That's the paradox: The more you let go of fear-based control, the more you can achieve—because you're no longer fighting reality, you're leading within it.

The Antidote to Fear— What Results in the Next Right Action

When fear rules our decisions, it reduces our potential and fractures our relationships. It keeps us separate and isolated. What is the antidote to fear? Get ready for the touchy-feely part; it's actually love.

You can't get to the next Right Action—the very point of the SHIFT process—without disengaging from fear. When you do, then the next Right Action suggests itself. Love is a simple four-letter word for a demanding and complicated idea. C. S. Lewis, in *The Four Loves*, distinguishes four kinds of love—affection (*storge*), friendship (*philia*), romantic love (*eros*), and selfless love (*agape*).

We are speaking of agape love, a deliberate commitment to another person's well-being—what Saint Thomas Aquinas called "to will the good of another." The antidote to self-will is the "other."

Throughout each day, your decision-maker—your mind—wavers between two voices. The ego's fearful shout is loud, urging you to grip harder, to hide, to fight, to blame—all repeated invitations to venture further into the Action Trap. But there's a quieter place inside you, call it intuition, spirit, or higher reasoning, that whispers about love, honesty, and abundance. When you choose to SHIFT, you consciously move away from fear's illusions (that you can—or must—control everything, that there's never enough, that what you want is the most important thing) and align with the thought system grounded in trust, collaboration, and love.

The self-based worldview insists on competition, scarcity, and control. Its inner script says:

- *Attack before being attacked.*
- *Control or be controlled.*
- *Keep secrets, or chaos will ensue.*

This mindset is fueled by the fear that, unless we grip tightly, we'll lose everything. In a fear-based workplace, employees hoard information, managers cling to rigid processes, and leaders gatekeep opportunities. People become self-protective instead of supportive, suspicious instead of trusting. It looks "productive" on the surface, but it erodes creativity and flattens people's spirits.

Love in the workplace offers a radical alternative. This worldview says:

- *I would rather give credit than receive it.*
- *I will trust before it is earned.*
- *Openness doesn't breed chaos—it creates clarity.*

In a culture where fear is tamed by love, competition still exists, but the competition is healthy, focused on bigger goals instead of petty rivalries. "Outperforming each other" is replaced by "supporting each other to outdo yesterday's best." Instead of fixating on the next quarter's numbers alone, we commit to fulfilling a greater purpose that the numbers are tracking toward.

Airbnb made love a company value. New York Life built an entire Super Bowl campaign around agape love, and yet whenever I (Jessica) explored the idea, I was swiftly told to quiet down. But in 2020, I began a master's in divinity at the Pacific School of Religion, and so I decided to dive into love once more.

I interviewed sixty CHROs to explore when and how genuine love manifests in the workplace. A recurring theme emerged. Employees experienced the deepest care and unity in one of two scenarios: during extreme crisis or extreme success. Layoffs, deaths, catastrophes—these were the moments that stripped away masks and laid bare our common humanity. People discovered that love (compassion, empathy, support) wasn't merely a "nice" concept; it was the only way they got through the storm. But they also showed love when they had remarkable success. The win brought out their inner "I love you, man."

And yet, love in the workplace remains taboo. We hesitate to say the word because it feels too personal, too emotional, too *vulnerable*. But if we strip away the corporate jargon, we're left with the simple truth: Love isn't just a feel-good concept. It's the vehicle to surrender.

Valley National Bank is a perfect example.

When Ira Robbins started at Valley National Bank thirty years ago, it was one of eight thousand commercial banks in the country. What set it apart wasn't just its financial performance—it was its *culture.* The bank held shared beliefs about the importance of its connection to the communities it served.

Then, in 2004, the leadership focus shifted from culture to strategy, from relationships to performance metrics. As the leadership focused on growth, they created new experiences for the employees, which led to new beliefs. Employees were still excellent at what they did, but they no longer felt the same bond with the institution or each other. The results reflected this shift—culture failed to shift along with strategy, and Ira Robbins, the CEO, realized they needed to get back to what mattered most.

Robbins puts it plainly: "Love was our value prop."

In addition to their focus on strategy, they doubled down on their culture of care coupled with accountability. It became Valley's greatest asset. In 2023, crisis struck—Silicon Valley Bank collapsed, throwing financial institutions into uncertainty. Valley National Bank didn't panic. Within three days, they had reached 70% of their commercial clients. While other banks struggled with damage control, Valley National Bank's employees were already in action, creating experiences for their clients that would drive the belief: We got you. They showed care, and they took accountability.

No MBA strategy or McKinsey playbook could replicate the deep cultural foundation that made that possible. Love—expressed through trust, service, and shared purpose.

The Valley National Bank story shatters a common misconception: that love in the workplace is soft, idealistic, or impractical. The opposite is true. Love is *harder* than fear-based leadership because it demands trust before it's earned. It demands giving credit rather than taking it. It demands giving up our natural tendency to put ourselves first.

The most radical truth is this: This is a binary choice. You are either operating from fear or you are operating from love. There is no middle ground.

That may feel uncomfortable—especially in a world that loves nuance. But the human experience is ultimately shaped by one of these two drivers. Every decision, every conversation, every experience you create either flows from fear (control, scarcity, self-protection) or love (trust, abundance, shared purpose). One contracts. The other expands. Fear-based cultures cling to scarcity, compliance, micromanagement, and short-term wins. Love-based cultures create the conditions for long-term excellence—where accountability isn't forced, it's embraced. Where people don't need to be pushed, because they're pulled by purpose.

It's not that love eliminates pressure. It transforms it. We believe that is why when the pressure is highest—during crises or moments of peak performance—love is what rises to the surface. So, the real leadership question isn't "How do we balance love and fear?" It's "Which one are you operating from?"

And if you've chosen love—really chosen it—then you know: It doesn't mean being soft. It doesn't mean avoiding hard conversations or lowering expectations. Love is not the absence of challenge. Love is the presence of responsibility. In fact, "Love is accountability."

That's a quote from Ron Alvesteffer, CEO of IT service provider Service Express and one of our accountability clients.

Ron didn't always lead this way. Early in his career, he was gripping tightly to results, pushing hard for performance, and unintentionally creating a culture of pressure rather than empowerment. He admits that at the time, he wasn't the leader he wanted to be—or even the person he wanted to be. Frustration was mounting, turnover was rising, and the business wasn't seeing the results he expected.

Then came a moment of transformation. Through feedback and self-reflection, Ron realized that his approach wasn't working—not just for his employees, but for himself. He had fallen into the Action Trap, believing that the only way to get better results was to demand more.

So, he made a shift. He let go and, in his words, he surrendered.

Instead of leading from fear, he focused on caring for others. He invested in people, understood their personal and professional goals, and took accountability to create an environment where they could thrive. Accountability was no longer a weapon; it was an act of care. As he puts it:

> Care doesn't mean not challenging people. It means celebrating what they're good at and coaching them where they need to grow. Love is accountability. I care about you enough to hold you accountable to the goals so that we—and you—can be successful here.

And the results followed.

Ron was promoted to president of Service Express, then later CEO. Under his leadership, the company grew from $3 million to over $300 million, with sights set on $1 billion. But more than the revenue, it was the culture that transformed. His team felt the difference so deeply that they made T-shirts reading, "Ron cares about me with the intensity of 1,000 suns."

This is what happens when leaders step out of fear and into love. It's not soft. It's not passive. It's demanding, disciplined, and transformative. Love fuels accountability, and accountability drives results. Ron's story is proof that when leaders stop gripping tightly and start *trusting deeply*, success follows.

But even when we choose love, we don't always remember it. We slip. We fall back into the Action Trap and we try to take back control and force our will on the universe.

I know I did. A few months after my Violeta moment of surrender, I found myself slipping back into old patterns. I wanted reassurance that I was still on the right path. Fear was creeping back into my life, and I found myself chasing again. I wanted another sign. Something magical to let me know I was going to be OK.

So, I asked the universe to send me a coin with my birth year on it. Then I went looking. I walked with my head down, scanning the pavement, picking up every coin I could find. For months I searched. None of them were right. The search became a fixation. My partner noticed. I told him I believed the coin would show up when my dad had something to tell me. I said it was about faith. But if I'm honest, it was about control.

And then one day, I came home, and he handed me a small box. Inside was a note: "I heard you were looking for one of these." And wrapped inside was a quarter—with my birth year on it. It stopped me in my tracks. It wasn't a cosmic sign. It wasn't a message from beyond. It was just a man who loves me and was paying attention. It was care. Presence. Love in its most ordinary form.

But maybe that's the point. Maybe love is the miracle.

That moment reminded me: Surrender isn't something you master. It's something you return to, especially when you forget. And when you do forget, it might not be the universe that reminds you. It might be someone you love. Or—it might be *you*.

Sometimes, you're the one who has to create the love. You make the call. You write the note. You give the feedback. You celebrate the effort. You tell the truth, even when it's uncomfortable.

That's the real lesson: Surrender isn't waiting for a sign. It's becoming one.

SHIFT Leads to Adaptability: The Real Driver of Growth

Love isn't just a feel-good concept. It's the turning point in the SHIFT process that allows us to get to the next Right Action. And when this happens, a new mindset evolves: one that is adaptable. The SHIFT process results in a culture of adaptability.

For years, we knew from experience that culture drove results, but we wanted to go deeper. We wanted hard data to prove it. So, we teamed up with Stanford to conduct the most comprehensive study ever done on how culture impacts business performance.

We already had a hypothesis: Purpose + Strategy + Culture = Results. This was our Results Equation. But we wanted proof. We took thirty years of Culture Partners' data—from clients like General Electric, Ocean Spray, and Chili's Bar and Grill—and analyzed 1,129 statements of espoused culture from organizations we had worked with. Each time a client hired us, they would tell us the kind of culture they wanted to create. This was our database. Then, we partnered with Stanford researchers, who ran a machine-learning analysis to categorize the most common culture themes organizations focused on.

The six dominant themes were:

1. Collaboration
2. Results-Oriented
3. Customer-Orientation
4. Innovation
5. Accountability
6. Trust

Then, the Stanford team proposed adding two more dimensions—adaptability and integrity—that they had seen emerge in previous studies. We had never had clients ask for those culture types, but we agreed.

With this framework, we set out to determine which of these eight culture types correlated most with business success. We gathered three years of performance data from 243 companies across multiple industries, from healthcare to retail to manufacturing. We dug into their purpose statements, their strategy, their culture, and of course, their results.

And when the results came in, we had our aha moment.

There was only one culture dimension that had a statistically significant correlation with revenue growth. It wasn't customer-orientation. It wasn't results-focus. It wasn't innovation.

It was adaptability.

Companies with adaptive cultures—organizations that could SHIFT their ways of thinking and acting in response to new strategies, crises, and market conditions—experienced an average revenue growth of 49.8% over three years.

Meanwhile, organizations that were fixated on a single culture type (like results-driven or customer-oriented) and Action Trapping their way toward a monolithic culture saw only 17% growth on average. *(To see the complete report, go to surrendertolead.com/resources or scan the QR code at the beginning of the book.)*

Let that sink in.

Companies that focused solely on execution, innovation, or customer service were *less* successful than those that built a culture of adaptability. The research was clear: Getting stuck in one type of culture leads to lower growth. In fact, organizations with adaptive cultures achieved 192% greater revenue growth than those that failed to adapt.

At first, we panicked a little. Very few companies had hired us and said, *"Help us be more adaptable."* It wasn't something people talked about in those words. But then we realized—we had been doing this all along.

Every company we worked with had the same problem: How do we shift culture from A to B so we can align with our evolving strategy to produce the results we need? And that's exactly what we had been helping them do, with the Results Pyramid.

The research exposed a fundamental flaw in the way most leaders think about culture.

Most leaders have a preferred culture type they hope to manifest by force of will. They like innovative cultures, or people-first cultures. Remember the Netflix Culture Deck, officially called "Netflix Culture: Freedom & Responsibility"? When it was first shared publicly in 2009, it caused quite a stir—this hugely disruptive and successful company was sharing its secrets to success. Sheryl Sandberg called it one of the most important documents ever to come out of Silicon Valley.[4]

This one deck inspired other companies to rethink their corporate cultures, emphasizing flexibility, performance, and accountability—all, of course, to no avail. What works for one company won't work for another.

This whole approach is just self-will in action. The leader believes that he or she knows the best way for everyone to think and act, and so they impose their will on the team. This is not surrender, and it doesn't work.

The Stanford research didn't just validate our work—it gave us a new North Star.

Stop trying to create the "perfect culture." Instead, build the capability to move culture as strategy evolves—to SHIFT the way leaders think and act as well as how those they lead respond, to arrive at the right place.

We are not the first to validate adaptability as a competitive differentiator in business. The Josh Bersin Company did extensive research in partnership with Gloat on a maturity model around organizational agility. They found that organizations that are the most dynamic, or adaptive, are seven times more successful at innovation, market leadership, and profitability than those that are not. In all his years of research, dynamic organizations—as Josh calls them—have the highest ROI of any maturity model he's ever studied. He argues that the problem most companies face is they see change as episodic. When a company needs to transform, they think of going from point A to point B. They hire consultants to figure out the difference between A and B, then they get to work changing roles, changing organizational structure, reskilling the people, and implementing training. Finally, anyone unable to move from A to B will be laid off. This is the Action Trap.

Josh argues that the research shows that to become dynamic, it all comes down to people. "There's a whole bunch of fear . . . that locks people in place. In a Dynamic Organization, we have to convince people that we as an organization are going to take care of them . . . . Irresistible leadership is not just having a vision and a real great strategy and talking people into doing things, but it's also knowing how to take care of people and support them as they make their personal journeys in the direction that the company is going."[5]

That's love, right action, and results.

The SHIFT to Clarity, Alignment, and Accountability

A sweeping shift from fear and control to love and abundance is at the heart of Surrendered Leadership. This new way of leading is more than just a feel-good approach; it creates the adaptability an organization needs to flourish, especially when strategies, technologies, and markets are in constant flux. Once you make the mental choice to SHIFT—deciding to surrender to the collective power of your people rather than relying on the illusion of total control—the next question is: What now? How do you, as a leader, create clarity, alignment, and accountability within your teams?

The Results Equation answers this question by weaving purpose, strategy, and culture into a unified framework to deliver extraordinary results. Your organization's purpose explains why you exist, your strategy outlines how you'll win, and your culture defines the way people think and act to deliver those results. According to our research, companies that achieve full alignment across these three elements experience an average of 44.5% revenue growth over three years—an extraordinary leap compared to the 10.7% observed in companies with partial or no alignment. It makes sense: A brilliant strategy can stall if no one's clear on how to execute it, or if people lack the collective mindset and motivation to see it through.

In the chapters that follow, we'll break down the practical steps to achieving this alignment. And along the way we'll tell you stories of companies that have shifted to surrender to drive results.

Wellby Financial, originally founded as JSC Federal Credit Union in 1961, began an ambitious transformation in late 2021— expanding beyond its legacy of serving the NASA workforce to embrace the broader Houston community. This bold transition required not just operational change but a cultural one as well.

Like many organizations navigating rapid growth and change, Wellby initially found itself caught in what's known as the Action Trap: a cycle of implementing new systems and processes to improve results—without first addressing the underlying experiences and beliefs shaping employee behavior. In other words, operational strategy was evolving, but culture was not yet aligned. As a result, member satisfaction wavered, employee retention became a growing concern, and internal confidence was tested.

The initial rollout of the new brand, systems, and infrastructure on October 10, 2021, became a defining moment—highlighting the need to move beyond activity and toward alignment. It became clear that sustainable transformation required more than action alone—it required a mindset shift.

As the new executive leadership team took shape, they brought a renewed sense of clarity and calm—one that didn't rely on control, urgency, or doing more, but on creating the space for others to lead. Rather than reacting to challenges with top-down directives, the team began modeling Surrendered Leadership: trusting in the collective intelligence of employees, listening deeply without defensiveness, and shifting the focus from simply fixing problems to inspiring shared ownership of results. This shift allowed leaders to move out of the action trap and into true alignment—moving from pressure to purpose, from control to connection. As they modeled transparency, vulnerability, and trust, a new tone was set across the organization: one where employees felt seen, heard, and empowered to act.

The focus then turned toward creating clarity, alignment, and accountability—foundational elements of meaningful cultural transformation that delivers results.

Clarity began with purpose. *Helping people prosper* became more than a corporate slogan—it became the lens through which every business decision was made. Teams aligned around a shared understanding of what success looked like: significantly improving member satisfaction, increasing employee engagement, and boosting employee retention across the organization. Clear key results and a focused strategy grounded the transformation.

With the strategy defined, the team turned to alignment. Using Culture Partners' Results Pyramid framework, Wellby prioritized creating experiences that shaped beliefs and inspired new ways of working. A culture rooted in feedback, continuous improvement, and shared accountability began to take hold—ensuring actions aligned to the strategy and delivered measurable results.

The final step was cultivating accountability—not through control, but through commitment. Leaders leaned into servant leadership, creating space for employees to voice challenges, offer solutions, and identify inefficiencies. Executives modeled vulnerability, owned outcomes, and listened with intention. This shift enabled a more agile, responsive, and empowered culture.

Among the many moments that reflect this cultural shift was the experience of a Wellby member who had recently moved to Finland and faced an issue connecting her authentication app to the Wellby mobile app. Although living abroad, the member retained Wellby accounts to manage US-based transactions. The issue was escalated to the digital solutions team, who coordinated a troubleshooting call at a time that worked for the member—3:00 a.m. Houston time. A Wellby employee stayed up in the early hours of the morning to personally walk through the steps and resolve the issue over the phone. The member was thrilled—not only that her issue was resolved, but that Wellby would go to such lengths, across time zones and outside regular hours, to support her experience. This commitment to ownership and service reinforced the culture Wellby had worked hard to build—where every employee feels empowered to act in the best interest of those they serve.

The impact of Wellby Financial's cultural transformation is measurable and meaningful. Over the last three years, member satisfaction—as reflected in the relationship Net Promoter Score (rNPS)—increased by nearly eighty-four points. Employee engagement has risen steadily, and perhaps most notably, the organization is already more than halfway toward its year-end 2027 goal of helping members prosper through achieving homeownership. These outcomes are the result of intentional clarity, alignment, and shared accountability across the organization.

Wellby's journey illustrates the cost of staying stuck in the Action Trap—and the power of escaping it. By focusing not just on strategy, but on aligning culture to purpose, the organization shifted from reactive action to intentional transformation. The result is a stronger, more resilient organization rooted in purpose and powered by people. While the journey isn't complete, Wellby continues to evolve—embracing progress, learning from the process, and celebrating success along the way. True transformation isn't a destination; it's a continued commitment to grow together.

Today, Wellby Financial is one of the largest credit unions in Houston, proudly serving more than 132,000 members across 22 branches with over $2.7 billion in assets. Recognized by Money.com, *Newsweek, USA Today,* and the *Houston Chronicle* as one of the best credit unions and top workplaces in the country, Wellby's transformation continues to be shaped by a deep commitment to its purpose: helping people prosper.

If we're talking your language and you'd like more resources on how you can embrace the shift to surrender, we have created a *SHIFT to Surrender Workbook* to help you put these principles into practice.

To get your copy, **visit surrendertolead.com/resources or scan the QR code at the beginning of the book.**

And if you're ready to create clarity, alignment, and accountability around your purpose, strategy, and culture to get results, keep reading. We'll show you how.

CHAPTER 3

THE SURRENDERED LEADER

Being a CEO is hard. Most of the job is problem-solving, which means dealing with things that are "not right" and need to be made "right." That can shape your worldview—fast.

There are two ways to look at this:

1. You get to be of service by helping fix problems.
2. You live in a world of broken things.

Same reality. But the mindset you bring to it changes everything.

The Command-and-Control Leader vs. the Surrendered Leader

There is a military-type Command-and-Control Leader inside each of us. This management mindset lives in self-will. And what that looks like, metaphorically, is living in a city under martial law.

When that leader takes over, they're hyperfocused on keeping us safe—and in business, "safe" means winning. That inner general believes he or she knows the path to results and will get there one way or another.

And like any good military commander, the Command-and-Control Leader has tools. Anger. Micromanagement. Perfectionism. Jealousy. Arrogance. People-pleasing. Finger-pointing. Impulsiveness. Fear. This Command-and-Control Leader builds walls, defends turf, and sees everyone as either an ally or a threat. It wants to control the outcome at all costs. And when the pressure rises (which, for leaders, is almost always), we default to martial law.

Inside us is also the Surrendered Leader. This leader doesn't react—it responds. It's grounded in trust, not fear. It sees the full picture, not just the threat. It doesn't force outcomes—it creates conditions. This is the adaptive leader. The one who leads from alignment, not anxiety. From curiosity, not control. This leader doesn't lean in; they let go.

But here's the catch: Just as with love and fear, only one can be in charge at a time.

When the Command-and-Control Leader takes over, it locks the Surrendered Leader in a room. "You stay here. It's not safe for you right now." The Command-and-Control Leader steps in and says, "Let me handle this." In certain moments, that makes sense. When you're being hunted by a tiger, you want the general in charge. Martial law is appropriate during war. But most of us aren't being hunted. We're just facing difficult conversations, disappointing results, or discomfort. And the Command-and-Control Leader goes way beyond keeping us safe—it starts trying to control everything.

So, the effective leader needs to be able to discern where you are in your business. Whether you need to be a wartime CEO because of the state of your business, or you are facing the business challenges leaders have faced for centuries. Too often leaders apply the Command-and-Control Leader mentality because of some short-term adversity—maybe they missed a quarter, or two, or even three. The reality is that this is part of being a leader. If you find yourself falling into Command-and-Control, you likely are overcompensating and have a scarcity mindset. It's exactly in these times, when the Command-and-Control Leader is screaming to get out, that you must summon and lean into your inner Surrendered Leader.

The Command-and-Control Leader is ego- and fear-driven, and therefore thinks the world is the problem. Action rules the day, regardless of whether it's the right action, so it gets to work rearranging things. The problem is never the world outside of you. The problem is inside yourself. The discontent, the anxiety, the prejudice about the way it should be—it's yours. It's all you. The Surrendered Leader, however, sees clearly. You don't change the world to feel OK. You change the way you relate to the world. The Surrendered Leader adapts; you connect and serve. You create an experience for others that comes from trust and abundance, rather than fear, ego, and control.

Again, this process is singular. It's either the Command-and-Control Leader or the Surrendered Leader; there is no place where both coexist.

Becoming the Surrendered Leader

So how do we put the Surrendered Leader back in charge?

You realize that you have a relationship with life.

The Surrendered Leader doesn't resist life—they use it. Every moment becomes fuel for growth. When something good happens, they embrace it fully. When something hard happens—stress, failure, conflict—they don't grip tighter. They pause. They feel it. And then they ask: What is this here to teach me?

That's the SHIFT in action.

- Stop fighting reality.
- Have faith that it's for your growth.
- Identify what's yours to own.
- Free yourself from fear.
- Take the next right action.

It's not about avoiding pain—it's about transforming it. You experience what's happening. You let go of what doesn't serve. You learn. And then you move forward lighter, wiser, and stronger. Over time, everything becomes part of the process. The joy, the mess, the setbacks—it's all part of your becoming. That's what a surrendered experience of life looks like. You stop resisting. You start evolving. And nothing is wasted.

This is surrender. It's not weakness—it's strength through presence. You don't numb. You don't control. You experience, release, and grow.

But when the ego is in charge, we live in fear. Fear of not getting what we want. Fear of losing what we have. Fear of what others think. And that fear drives our self-will. It drives the manager mindset.

In those moments, the Command-and-Control Leader doesn't relate to life—it relates to a mental blueprint of how life should be. And it resents anything that doesn't fit.

The tools of the Command-and-Control Leader—fear, anger, blame, control, manipulation—might have served you in the past. But the question is: Are you willing to let them go? That is the question you have to ask yourself. The Surrendered Leader doesn't need different tools; they just need to let go of the counterproductive tools that the Command-and-Control Leader uses.

Get a Post-it note right now and write down, "Which leader is in charge?" Put it somewhere on your desk and remind yourself every day to choose the Surrendered Leader within.

The Truth About Results

When we fixate on outcomes, we activate fear. And fear leads to dysfunction. You can see it in your own life. You can see it in your company. You can see it in the system.

As a leader, if you're trying to fix everything outside of you so you feel OK inside, you will always be exhausted. But if you change your inner condition, the outer world begins to change too—because your perspective shifts. Gratitude is one tool for that shift. So is faith. So is surrender.

I (Joe) had to put all three to work after we submitted this book to the publisher. Just a few days after submitting the final manuscript, I had a serious bicycle accident in the final miles of a 100-mile training ride, which put me in the hospital for six days. My injuries were substantial: concussion, broken collarbone (which required surgery), broken scapula, eight broken ribs, a collapsed lung, a fractured pelvis, and a whole lotta road rash.

There was so much going on in our business; we were in the middle of a buying process (we are backed by private equity) with new investors, and of course the quarter results are always crucial during this process. Here I was in one of the most vulnerable and challenging experiences of my life. I was forced to release everything.

This experience was the ultimate test of surrender. I was in constant pain and couldn't even breathe without assistance. Sleep in the first eight weeks was especially challenging, and my normal routines in work and life were thrown into a complete tailspin. I wanted to lead, but my body and mind were struggling to focus and keep up. The Command-and-Control Leader wanted to panic, but the Surrendered Leader knew that there's nothing to fix. Just be. Let go. Learn.

While I practiced being the Surrendered Leader for many years, this took it to another level I never thought possible! I went deep into gratitude and abundance and surrendered to the trust that my team would step forward to lead where I couldn't. I had faith that the results would come. Little did I know, this was all part of the plan.

Before the accident, I had witnessed their capability daily. I knew I could rely on them, and this was the time to trust. My team had clarity, and they were aligned and were taking full account- ability. Every experience they created and action they were taking was 100 percent focused on our vision of impacting five million lives in 2025 with the work we do. The Surrendered Leader was alive, well, and thriving! And the results? Well, they came like never before: breaking records while achieving over 100 percent year-over-year top-line growth!

The thing about surrender is you can't fake it. You either embrace it or you don't. You can't pretend to trust your team while secretly micromanaging every detail. Accountability extends to moments of vulnerability as well. How can you build trust within your team or yourself if you deny struggles or exert control on every single detail?

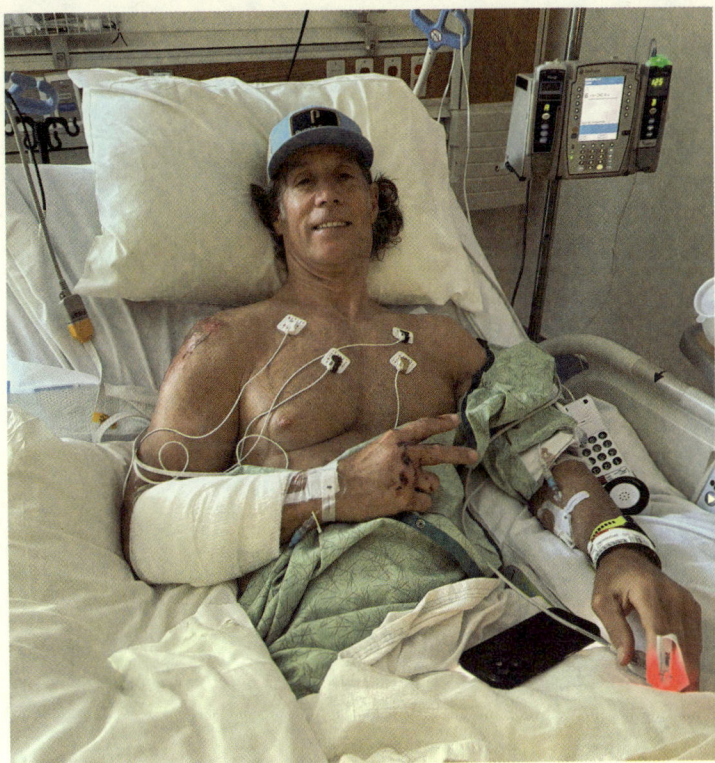

During my recovery, I had to be honest with myself about what I could handle and to not hesitate to ask for assistance when needed (a lesson I had to learn). In this moment, the Command-and-Control Leader would want to push, take care of everything, and hide any sign of weakness—even at the expense of their own health. But the Surrendered Leader observes and knows when to listen and be flexible.

Surrendering fosters resilience and strength. When people see you lead from a place of vulnerability, honesty, and authenticity, and by experiencing your trust in them, they will connect to your shared purpose and ultimately flourish, exceeding your expectations and achieving results you never thought possible (without you ☺). This is the lived experience of the Surrendered Leader.

The CEO of data-storage giant Seagate had a sign in his office that said: "If you don't live it, you don't believe it." You can't talk about accountability while controlling every outcome. You have to live it. And when you do, your people will too.

The Surrendered Leader doesn't control actions. They create conditions. They build environments where the right actions emerge, not from fear but from belief.

In these next three sections, we'll show you a step-by-step process for how to be the Surrendered Leader.

Before you dive in, be sure to take our Surrendered Leader Assessment. This will provide you with a better understanding of where you currently stand as a leader on the surrender spectrum.

To take the assessment, visit surrendertolead.com/resources.

PART ONE

CLARITY

CHAPTER 4

THE RESULTS EQUATION

Imagine you're watching *Night of the Living Dead*, the classic 1960s zombie thriller. The tension is suffocating—the undead are clawing at the doors, survivors are barricading themselves inside, and panic is setting in. But something is off. The eerie black-and-white visuals remain, the desperate dialogue is intact—but the soundtrack? Instead of an ominous, heart-pounding score, the theater fills with the cheerful, whimsical tunes of *The Wizard of Oz*.

Suddenly, the fear evaporates. It doesn't matter how dire the situation looks or how much the characters scream for their lives—when the music is lighthearted and full of wonder, the stakes feel nonexistent. The entire tone of the film is undermined.

Or imagine the opposite: The dialogue is still from *Night of the Living Dead*, the soundtrack is eerie and foreboding—but the visuals have been swapped for *The Wizard of Oz*. Dorothy, Toto, and the Tin Man are delivering lines about impending doom while skipping down the Yellow Brick Road. It's disorienting, absurd, and completely ineffective.

This is exactly what happens when **purpose, strategy, and culture** aren't aligned.

- **The dialogue (Purpose):** This is the core message of the movie—why it exists, what it's trying to say. In a business, it's the company's deeper mission and reason for being.
- **The visuals (Strategy):** This is how the story unfolds—the way it's structured, the way events play out to bring the message to life. In business, strategy is the execution plan, the tangible steps designed to deliver on the company's purpose.
- **The soundtrack (Culture):** This is what gives the story emotional weight. The right soundtrack enhances every scene, making the audience feel what they're supposed to feel. In business, culture works the same way—it creates the energy, emotion, and momentum behind execution.

If any of these elements are misaligned, the entire experience collapses. A company might have a bold, inspiring purpose, but if its strategy doesn't match the vision, or if the culture sends an entirely different emotional signal, the result is confusion, inconsistency, and disengagement.

That's why alignment matters so much. It's not just about having the right components—it's about having them work in harmony. And I (Jessica) didn't fully understand the power of this alignment until I met Shawn Price.

Shawn's friends called him a real-life James Bond. Not only was he a polished executive who dressed to the nines; he was a thrill-seeker, a competitor, a man who lived at full speed. Whether racing a Porsche GT3 in the Rolex twenty-four-hour Daytona race, tackling the grueling 6,000-mile Paris-to-Dakar motorcycle rally, or leading global cloud transformations, Shawn Price had one gear: forward. And when he arrived at Oracle, he brought that same intensity.

Price was hired as part of a company-wide transformation imperative that was as audacious as any of his races—turning a legacy on-premise technology giant into a cloud-first company. It was 2014. Oracle had around 120,000 employees and revenue of $38 billion. But despite its size, it was facing fierce competition from the likes of Salesforce and Workday, which were born in the cloud. Just a month before Price was hired, Oracle co-CEO Mark Hurd said on a conference call that the company was on track to post $2 billion in cloud revenue—which was large but still would have been only 5% of its total business at the time (and half of Salesforce revenue). Cloud was clearly the future, but smaller competitors had a head start. Today, companies face a similar crossroads with AI. Just as companies must rapidly shift to embrace AI, they are already competing against AI-first disruptors.

I was an organizational development consultant at Oracle, and as luck would have it, I was assigned to Shawn's team to help drive the company's transition to the cloud. My role was to work closely with leaders like Shawn to ensure that employees not only understood the strategic imperative but also embraced the mindset shift required to win. It was a front-row seat to one of the most ambitious transformations in tech, and it shaped my perspective on how culture drives results.

For three days, we sat huddled in a conference room at Oracle's Redwood Shores, California, headquarters. Shawn was brilliant with deep expertise, having just served as the head of the cloud business at SAP. The more we discussed, the more we realized the sheer complexity of what lay ahead. This wasn't just about strategy or even technology. This was about change—fundamental, radical, systemic change. We weren't just rolling out a new product; we were rewiring an entire way of thinking.

At the time, many Oracle employees, let alone customers, didn't even fully understand what the cloud was. The hurdles were significant. Oracle had a rudimentary cloud sales process that wasn't built for enterprise or volume, not enough sales reps were cloud-first, and the first-line sales managers lacked cloud sales experience. There was limited ability to generate quality pipeline and a slow, complex negotiation and contracting process.

Shawn was an idea machine—constantly throwing out insights, strategies, and solutions. He was a firehose of innovation and complexity. Every conversation led to another layer, another challenge, another opportunity. One moment we were untangling how to shift a sales force trained to sell in the language of products into one that sold in the language of the customer. The next we were wrestling with the friction of legacy contract structures before moving on to reeducating customers on the ecosystem support model. Every decision had ripple effects—on pricing, partnerships, customer success, and job roles. Shawn had ideas and strategies for all of them, but instead of clarity, we were sinking deeper into the chaos.

I could feel my frustration building. And I could see it in him too—he wasn't getting the alignment he needed, and I wasn't getting the clarity I needed. The room felt heavier with every passing minute, the weight of 120,000 people who would need to understand and execute this transformation pressing down on us.

Finally, after another whirlwind exchange that led us back into the weeds, I let out a sigh, rubbed my temples, and just said, "Shawn—why are you here?"

He paused, exhaled, and said, "I'm here to create a cloud company with non-cloud DNA."

I wrote that down.

"And what's the goal?" I asked.

"To maximize cloud bookings."

I wrote it down and kept asking about the fundamentals. What will we measure? How will we do it? And finally, what shifts in mindset will we need to succeed?

He answered, and I wrote everything down. Then I distilled it onto one slide. That was it. The single core narrative of who we were, why we existed, how we were going to do it, and the way to get it done. This one slide was the key to clarity and a guiding light for alignment and accountability organizationwide. This was the birth of the Results Equation.

Two years later, Shawn Price passed away at the age of fifty-three. His death was a shock, but his professional legacy was undeniable. In announcing his passing, Mark Hurd said: "Two years ago, Shawn joined Oracle to help lead our global transformation to cloud. He became an instant catalyst and introduced ideas and practices to help us compete more effectively and win in cloud. He was an exceptional, passionate individual who lived life to the fullest with his many adventures, and he helped our company achieve great cloud success."[6]

And he did. By fiscal year 2024, Oracle's cloud services and license support revenue had skyrocketed to $39.4 billion, making up 74% of the company's total $53 billion in revenue.[7] The transformation wasn't just a strategic pivot—it was a complete reinvention of Oracle's DNA.

He did it. He changed the company's DNA.

* * *

There's a truth that executives love to ignore: Organizations are drowning in unnecessary complexity. They bury themselves beneath jargon-laden strategic frameworks, ambiguous mission statements, product road maps, and bureaucratic labyrinths of processes, KPIs, and dashboards. But complexity is not sophistication—it is dysfunction.

While most organizations have a purpose, strategy, culture, and results they hope to achieve, they struggle because these elements are not clear or aligned.

The purpose (or mission) statement was probably written years ago—some ornate sentence concocted by the founders, or a hard-hitting new tagline written by the new CEO making their mark. The strategy comes from a big-name consulting company for a fine penny, or it was hashed out at an executive offsite in Napa. Oftentimes there is no strategy, and what companies think is their strategy is really just a product road map. And culture? That's delegated to HR. Employee engagement surveys and value statements with a dash of "the way we do things around here."

The Results Equation connects the dots. It brings all of these elements together into one cohesive framework that aligns purpose, strategy, culture, and results into a scalable vision (which we refer to as R2 Vision and will say more about later) that helps stitch the entire equation together. Instead of scattered initiatives developed independently and misaligned priorities, the Results Equation creates a clear, measurable path forward. It forces leaders to distill complexity into clarity, stripping away the noise and focusing on what truly drives success. Our research with Stanford showed that organizations fully aligned across purpose, strategy, and culture saw 316% greater revenue growth than those with partial or no alignment.

At its core, the Results Equation answers five fundamental questions:

1. **Why do we exist? (Purpose):** The deeper reason the organization exists, beyond just making money.
2. **What are we trying to achieve? (Vision):** The tangible, measurable outcome that will define our success in the long-term—three to five years.
3. **What will we measure? (Key Results):** The metrics that ensure accountability and progress along the way in the short term.
4. **How will we get there? (Strategic Drivers):** The big strategic bets we've made as a team to differentiate and win.
5. **What is the way we work? (Cultural Beliefs):** The shared beliefs that drive how we execute our strategy and achieve our vision.

Visually, it looks like this:

Purpose			
R2/Vision			
Key Results			
Strategic Drivers			
Cultural Beliefs			

(To download a Results Equation Builder,
go to surrendertolead.com/resources or scan the
QR code at the beginning of the book.)

When these elements are misaligned, companies spin in circles—caught in a cycle of ineffective meetings, conflicting priorities, and initiatives that never gain traction. It's like the *Night of the Living Dead* visuals set to Wizard of Oz music.

When I (Joe) saw the Results Equation come together for the first time, I was struck by its simplicity. It made intuitive sense to me—a simple bridge between strategy and execution that so many companies failed to cross. I believed immediately that this was something our clients would derive tremendous value from and could positively impact millions of lives.

Culture Partners had a long history of helping companies identify their Key Results and activating results through shared cultural beliefs, but we were missing the critical elements of purpose and strategy that created a whole solution. Jessica's company had those critical elements to complete the solution. So, we made it official—bringing Jessica and her work into our business to help even more organizations transform the way they think and act to get results.

We started using the Results Equation right away, and we got results fast. But I've been in business long enough to know that early success can sometimes be luck. I have a saying: "One win is a data point. Two is interesting. And three is a trend."

After three client successes, I wanted to be sure. Was this a repeatable framework? Could it scale? Could it be measured, validated, and proven to work across industries? We had proven it in the real world with our clients. That's when Jessica and I agreed to challenge our thesis with research. It wasn't enough for us to just believe in. We wanted undeniable proof.

As we reached out to potential research partners, we realized that most of them were in the business of marketing. We were promised that they could validate our real-world client success with research. But we didn't want to just "validate" our client results; we wanted to challenge them, and we wanted real data, real case studies, and a rigorous analysis that could stand up to scrutiny. We were willing to be proven wrong if that was the truth. The SHIFT mindset was our guiding principle:

1. **We (S)topped fighting reality.** We didn't want to manipulate the truth. We wanted to live in the truth.
2. **We (H)ad faith.** Even if the Results Equation did not pass muster, we knew we would learn something and be able to pivot accordingly.
3. **We (I)dentified what we could control.** We could operate with integrity and do the research with a trusted partner.
4. **We (F)reed ourselves from fear.** We let go of our need to be right, and we thought of our clients first. We wanted to serve them in the best way possible.
5. **We (T)ook the next right action.** We partnered with Stanford Graduate School of Business.

And the shift worked. What we found blew us away. Not only did it confirm what we had already experienced firsthand: the Results Equation drove results. Looking at 243 companies across all industries and sizes, those that had full alignment across their purpose, strategy, and culture saw 44.5% revenue growth over three years, compared to just 10.7% for those that were not aligned. The results were astonishing! But the aha moment for us was realizing exactly why it drove results.

And there it was, simple yet profound.

Why? Because strategy evolves. Markets change. New technologies appear. Pandemics happen. CEOs leave, sometimes unexpectedly. Leaders who see culture as a static entity, separate from purpose and strategy, inevitably get trapped. The Results Equation is dynamic. When strategy changes, culture must shift to align with it.

Here's the key insight on why it works: Your purpose, strategy, and culture cannot exist independently if you want sustained growth. Treating them separately is precisely how most companies go wrong. They set purpose once (with one group of people), then rewrite strategy in annual retreats (with another group of people), and delegate culture to HR (with yet another group of people)—ignoring the need for ongoing, adaptive alignment.

The Results Equation worksheet is a living document that breathes every week, every quarter, and every year. This is not something you paint on the wall and forget about. As shifts take place, the entire framework shifts together. Nothing is siloed.

Suncoast Credit Union, based in Tampa, Florida, is a client that we can all learn from.

When we were brought in, Suncoast was already considered a great place to work. Employees consistently praised its supportive atmosphere, and customers—whom Suncoast calls "members"—expressed high satisfaction year after year. With over 1.1 million members and a team of 2,500 employees, Suncoast had already earned its place as a pillar among Florida's credit unions.

But Suncoast had bold expansion plans, and its leaders are well aware that growth creates challenges that can chip away at the strength of an organization. Suncoast set out to double its membership to 2.5 million by 2030 and achieve an ambitious annual growth rate of 11%. Hence, the company needed a strategic culture shift so it could adapt as it expands and experiences growing pains.

Put simply, the status quo wasn't an option. Suncoast needed a framework to ensure new employees would assimilate into their culture rather than dilute it. This meant aligning everyone—new and existing employees alike—with the company's purpose, strategy, culture, and results.

Suncoast also wanted to ensure that internal systems, such as technology, decision-making, and operational processes, supported their culture rather than contradicting it. For example, outdated approval systems that slowed decision-making were reassessed to align with their emphasis on empowerment and agility.

After partnering with us, they came up with their Results Equation:

Suncoast's Results Equation

Purpose	Improve the Financial Lives of Our Members		
R2/Vision	Reach 2.5M Members by 2030		
Key Results	Annual Member Growth of 11%	Net Promoter Score of 80%	App Rating of 4.80
Strategic Drivers	Growth Through Price & Financial Wellness	Be the Member's Advocate	Be Envied in Digital Delivery
Cultural Beliefs	**GOT IT** I confidently own every member & employee experience & find solutions.	**DO IT** I make decisions. I am trusted and supported. My voice matters.	**GROW IT** I thrive on opportunity that ignites growth.

This one sheet is the script for the story of who they are.

Look around your company right now and ask yourself:

- Is our purpose clear, inspiring, and connected to strategy and culture?
- Is our strategy simple enough for everyone to understand and act on immediately?
- Is our culture just memorialized, or is it operationalized— do people actually think and act consistently with our strategic direction?

If the answer isn't a clear yes, then your complexity may be strangling your growth.

Your job now, today, is straightforward: Sit down with your team and build your Results Equation. You do not need to be the CEO of your company to have a Results Equation. Leaders at any level can create a Results Equation for their team. This clarity isn't just nice to have—it's essential for growth.

The chapters ahead will walk you through each element of the Results Equation in detail, giving you practical steps, case studies, and actionable insights to achieve true clarity, alignment, and accountability. By doing this, you'll escape the complexity trap, align your entire organization, and drive results like never before.

You don't have to choose between simplicity and scale. You need simplicity to scale. This is how you'll win. We are writing this book because when you find something that works, you don't just use it—you champion it. We are evangelists. But evangelism alone isn't enough. Transformation demands a shift—from frustration to acceptance, from hesitation to conviction, from overwhelm to focus, from fear to love, from passive participation to full accountability. The Results Equation isn't just a framework; it's a call to lead differently.

The path to results starts now. Let's shift.

CHAPTER 5

PURPOSE

In 2015, Sacramento, California, went silent.

For the first time in decades, the city had no live orchestral music. The Sacramento Philharmonic and the Sacramento Opera—two beloved local institutions—had run out of funding. They had spent years scraping by, hosting galas, chasing big donors, cutting corners where they could. But it wasn't enough. Donations had dried up, attendance had dwindled, and both organizations faced an existential crisis. One by one, the lights went out and board members left. The silence was deafening.

As a last-ditch effort, the remaining board members of the two struggling organizations decided to merge and recruit. I (Jessica) was asked to join along with a few other new recruits in an effort to breathe new life (and new pocketbooks) into a dying organization. The hope was that combining resources would save them. As a former theater major and lover of live music, I was happy to serve, but my pocketbook was not the saving grace they might have hoped. If I couldn't contribute financially, I needed to find another way to be useful. Around that time, I had just started working with Shawn Price at Oracle. Perhaps, I thought, I could offer a path to clarity.

At my first board meeting, I met the twelve other board members and the interim CEO. We were starting from scratch and needed a path forward. I asked a simple question:

"What is the mission statement of the Philharmonic? Or the Opera?"

Silence.

These were people who had poured tens of thousands of their own dollars into the organization. People who had spent years advocating for the arts. And yet, not a single person could recall the mission statement of the organizations they had been fighting to save.

I'm asking you right now, dear reader, do you know your organization's mission statement by heart? No peeking at your company's intranet.

I would bet the majority of readers don't. Seventy-six percent of the executive leadership teams we work with do not have clarity, alignment, and accountability on their purpose. Think about that for a moment. This is the top of the organization, and they are not clear on why the company exists? If the ten executives who lead a company are not clear, how can you expect tens of thousands or even a hundred employees to be clear on why the company they work for exists? Why the work they do matters?

We pulled up an old slide deck and found the old mission statements. They were like most mission statements—a long, bloated attempt to be everything to everyone. The Philharmonic's read something like:

The Sacramento Philharmonic engages, inspires, and unites diverse communities across the Sacramento area through outstanding music performances and innovative education programs.

Meanwhile, the Opera's was:

We gather and inspire audiences, artists, and collaborators to create shared opera experiences that enliven and connect us all, enhancing the cultural landscape of the beautiful region.

They weren't wrong. They were just . . . too much. They crammed in the purpose, the audience, the strategy, and even elements of the culture. They were beautifully written; they were utterly forgettable.

So, I asked another question: "Why are we here?"

At first, the answers were long-winded, filled with arts jargon and passionate pleas about cultural significance. Then we started writing words on the whiteboard. But I kept pushing. "No," I said, "why are we here? What is the one, simple reason we exist?"

After much debate, we got it down to five words: *We engage the community with music.*

That was it. That was our purpose. And the purpose statement changed everything.

Once we had clarity, everything else became easier. Every decision, every strategy, every dollar spent had to align with that purpose. When someone suggested holding concerts outdoors, we asked: Does it help us engage the community with music? If yes, we did it. When someone proposed a concert featuring only Queen songs, some of the board members balked. Then we asked the same question. When we considered bringing in schools to expose kids to the arts, we asked it again.

Instead of chasing prestige or clinging to tradition for tradition's sake, we focused on engaging the community with music. When board members asked donors to give, they shared the purpose statement. When programs were written, we shared the purpose statement. Everyone knew the purpose statement by heart because it was simple and it was clear.

The city responded. The next season, in 2016, the Sacramento Philharmonic and Opera made its return. Audiences returned, donations followed, and the energy shifted from survival mode to a provider of music, of joy, of engaging the community. More than 5,000 members of the community attended concerts that season. Today, they engage over 50,000 people a year. They are thriving—not because they got lucky, but because they got clarity.

This story echoes a broader truth supported by research: Purpose matters. McKinsey & Company reports that employees who find meaning in their work are more productive and resilient.[8] And Gartner emphasizes that today's workforce craves purpose at work.[9] Purpose isn't a buzzword—it's a performance driver.

One powerful business case for purpose comes from Thrive Market. The company was founded with a singular mission: "to make healthy and sustainable living easy and affordable for everyone." This mission was deeply personal for Nick Green, the cofounder and CEO, who recalled watching his mom struggle to access healthy food while raising him in the Midwest. That experience shaped the reason he built Thrive Market—and it became the organization's North Star.

"We found that the more we leaned into the mission, the more loyalty our members had for us," Nick shared. "The higher our renewal rates ended up being, and that drives actually the major source of our profitability."

When traditional VCs rejected their pitch—over a hundred times, Nick and his cofounders didn't back down. The VC "experts" consistently dismissed their model, claiming that anyone who wanted healthy food would just shop at Whole Foods. They couldn't see beyond their own coastal urban bubbles and failed to grasp the reality that most Americans didn't live near a Whole Foods—or couldn't afford it even if they did. To the VCs, the problem Thrive Market was solving didn't exist. But to Nick, the mission was personal. That disconnect between investor perception and lived experience only strengthened his commitment. Instead of compromising their purpose to fit a traditional growth story, they raised funds from over 150 aligned influencers who understood the mission, believed in it, and were willing to invest.

To align with sustainable living, they chose to implement carbon-neutral shipping from day one, even when it cost more. Over time, they invested in zero-waste fulfillment centers, plastic-neutral packaging, and free memberships for low-income families. At every step, they made choices rooted in purpose, not profit.

The result? Today, Thrive Market serves over 1.6 million members and generates half a billion in revenue. Their members are also their most powerful marketing engine—referrals from loyal users remain their number one source of growth. Purpose didn't cost them growth—it fueled it.

And Thrive Market is far from alone. The data is piling up: Purpose is good business.

In global leadership consulting firm DDI's "2018 Global Leadership Forecast" (compiled in collaboration with The Conference Board and EY), companies that both defined and acted with a clear sense of purpose outperformed financial markets by 42%. But those that merely talked the talk—with a mission statement on the wall but no action—performed no better than average. And organizations without any sense of purpose? They underperformed by 42%.[10]

Harvard Business Review chronicled DTE Energy's turnaround after the 2008 financial crisis. CEO Gerry Anderson redefined the company's purpose as: *We serve with our energy, the lifeblood of communities and the engine of progress.* He embedded that purpose into everything—from meetings to employee training to sing-alongs. The result? DTE's stock price more than tripled over the next nine years.[11]

A *Harvard Business Review Analytic Services* report, published in partnership with EY's Beacon Institute, found compelling evidence that purpose pays off. Among companies that prioritized both defining and acting on their organizational purpose, 58% experienced revenue growth of 10% or more over a three-year period. In stark contrast, 42% of the laggards—those either doing nothing or merely thinking about purpose—reported flat or declining revenue during the same time. The takeaway is clear: Purpose isn't just inspirational—it's operational. And it drives results.[12]

So why don't more companies operate this way? Pride. Fear. Misconceptions. Some executives still view purpose as "soft," or something you can't measure. Some even scoff at it—calling it "fluff" or "PR." But the data tells a different story. Purpose isn't fluff. It's a winning strategy.

A great purpose statement isn't just a line in a corporate document—it's the heartbeat of an organization. It should inspire, giving people a reason to care. It should be simple, because if no one remembers it, it's useless. And it should be meaningful, capturing the core reason the organization exists. It should have nothing to do with money, measurement, strategy, culture, stakeholders, or marketing.

And here's the big one: It should be no more than six words.

Anything longer is trying to do too much. It's likely spilling over into other elements of the Results Equation—R2 Vision, Key Results, Strategic Drivers, or Cultural Beliefs. A crucial distinction: A purpose is not a strategy. It's not a vision. It's not a list of goals or a marketing tagline. A purpose is the reason you wake up in the morning and care.

Look at some of the strongest purpose statements out there. Tesla's is *Accelerate the world's transition to sustainable energy*. Technically, it's seven words. Close enough. Nike keeps it even tighter: *Bring inspiration and innovation to athletes*. Airbnb? *Create a world where anyone belongs*. These statements don't mention revenue, product lines, or market conditions. They are clear, simple, and timeless. They answer the one essential question: *Why are we here?*

Now, it's your turn. Take a hard look at your purpose statement. Is it clear? Is it simple? Could everyone in your organization commit it to memory? If not, it's time to cut the fluff. Strip it down to six words. And if your organization doesn't have one, start with the only question that matters: *Why* are we here? Keep pushing until you land on something that's inspiring, simple, and meaningful.

Clarity of purpose is the foundation. But it's just the beginning. Once you know why you're here, the next step is defining how you will know if you got there. That's where vision comes in. A great vision statement takes the energy of purpose and points it toward a future worth striving for.

In the next chapter, we'll explore how to craft a vision that creates clarity and aligns with purpose to drive momentum. Knowing why you exist is powerful—but knowing what the finish line looks like is what turns purpose into progress.

CHAPTER 6

R2 VISION

To talk about vision, we need to revisit the Results Pyramid—the foundation of how organizations drive results.

At Culture Partners, we teach that results don't come from mandates or directives. You cannot exert your will onto your team and expect to drive transformative growth.

Too many leaders fall into the Action Trap—focusing on programs, policy changes, initiatives, or technology, thinking these will improve results. And they will, to an extent. But the Surrendered Leader knows that a more powerful way to drive results is through a shift in thinking.

True leadership is about having faith in the power of your people. Instead of micromanaging actions or enforcing rigid processes, the best leaders focus on creating the right experiences—because experiences shape beliefs, and beliefs drive action. And after all, all you can control is the experiences you create for others.

This is the basis of the Results Pyramid:

Experiences shape beliefs.
Beliefs drive actions.
Actions produce results.

The first role of a leader is to create clarity. Once you have clarity on your why, the next step is to establish a single, measurable finish line—a clear, meaningful target that will determine whether you've successfully lived out your why over the next three to five years. This is your vision.

One of the first research projects I (Jessica) did at Culture Partners was aimed at understanding what truly creates strong cultures in organizations. We wanted to move beyond anecdotal evidence and quantify the impact of different factors within the Results Pyramid. To do this, we used data from our Culture Assessment, which gathers insights from our clients around each element of the Results Pyramid to help drive alignment (we will get to alignment in part 2). Our analysis included nearly 5,000 employees across twenty-six organizations, examining how experiences, beliefs, actions, and results interact to shape culture.

Our findings were striking. The single most impactful factor in strengthening workplace culture, and therefore alignment, was clarity of results. Organizations with clearly defined results experienced a 44% increase in culture strength. When combined with the other levels of the Results Pyramid, culture strength improved by 62%.

This research reinforces what we've seen time and again: The most effective leaders don't just paint a vague vision of the future; they define a tangible, measurable future state—one that employees can rally around. Having a clear vision puts the employees first by giving them a destination worth striving for. Set a clear finish line because when people have clarity, they don't just comply—they commit.

To clarify the difference between a vague vision statement and a compelling one, we use the language of the Results Pyramid.

The results you are achieving today are called R1—your day-one results. These results come from your current actions, which are shaped by your existing beliefs and experiences. This collective way of thinking and acting is what defines your current culture, or C1.

A strong vision statement provides a clear picture of R2—the future results you want to achieve. However, your current culture (C1) cannot support your future results (R2). C1 is perfectly aligned with R1, not R2. The ways of thinking and acting you're using today get you the results of today. To reach R2, your culture must evolve from C1 to C2—a new set of experiences, beliefs, and actions that can sustain your vision for the future. You have to shift your culture to shift your results.

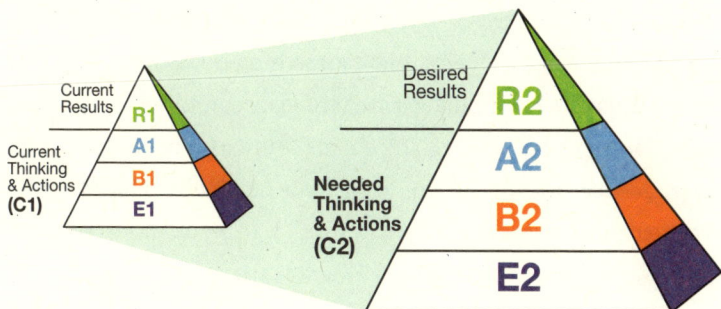

It's important to note that most of our clients don't have bad cultures (C1) or bad results (R1). In fact, when one hired us, they had just wrapped up their thirty-seventh consecutive "best year ever." But they recognized, as the saying goes in our line of work, that "what got us here won't get us there." Their current culture (C1) was perfectly designed to achieve their current success (R1), but it wasn't built to achieve their future vision (R2).

That's the challenge of transformation: The thinking and actions that created today's success aren't enough to create tomorrow's breakthrough.

Crafting a clear and compelling R2 vision statement is no small task. First and foremost, it needs a deadline and a measurable outcome. But that alone isn't enough. At Culture Partners, we faced this challenge firsthand.

When I (Joe) joined Culture Partners in August 2020, the company was in crisis. COVID-19 had hit us hard. At the time, 100% of our client delivery was in person, and when the world shut down, so did our revenue stream. From the first quarter to the second quarter of 2020, revenue dropped 82% and bookings dropped by 83%. The company was reeling, and I was brought in by the private equity partners HKW to lead the climb—not just back to where we were, but beyond.

Despite the challenges, I saw something powerful: a company with incredible intellectual property, deeply committed employees, and a true passion for serving clients. But I also believed that we needed to adapt, or we would die. We needed to adapt both in strategy and culture.

When setting goals (R2 or Key Results), it's best to reverse-engineer the win—to look ahead, imagine standing at the finish line and looking back. Imagine it is the last day of the year and you are walking out the door. What would you hope to have accomplished so that whoever came in to take your place would feel like you had set them up for success? If you quit your job the day you reach the finish line, what would make your successor say, "Wow, that leader left a legacy of execution." That is your goal. Set that goal even though you aren't leaving. That is what coming from love looks like when target setting. That's what being in service means.

With that mindset, we set our target: 250% growth by 2025.

It was ambitious, clear, and measurable. When we rolled it out to the team, there was some enthusiasm around the idea of growth. But there was a problem—it wasn't inspiring. HKW was certainly excited about it, but to our employees, it wasn't particularly meaningful. And I don't blame them; it is hard to get inspired by a revenue target.

After a year or so, the R2 Vision kept feeling like a corporate objective rather than a vision that would inspire both our employees and our clients to a place of greatness. It was a number on a spreadsheet, not a rallying cry. And that was the problem—it lacked heart. While executives and investors cared about revenue, our employees needed something deeper, something that connected to their sense of purpose. Something that connected to our purpose.

So, we went back to the whiteboard. We asked ourselves: What does winning look like beyond the balance sheet? We needed a vision that captured not just financial growth but also the kind of company we wanted to become—one that made an undeniable impact on our clients, our people, and the industry as a whole.

I asked myself how we might lean into love even more.

That's when the shift happened. I realized that 250% growth wasn't just a number—it was a way to measure how much of an impact we were having on the world with our work. We weren't chasing revenue for the sake of financial gain; we were trying to make an impact on people's lives.

As evangelists, we believe that workplace culture isn't just a business issue—it's a human one. When people are fulfilled at work, they don't just perform better; they live better. We want to unleash the power of culture to inspire people and organizations to reach their full potential. If we can do that, the impact will not just make a difference to our clients, it will ripple outward—into families, communities, and even future generations.

This is not just about feeling good. It's about results. When people are aligned and engaged in meaningful work, they are more productive, creative, committed, and ultimately happier. This is what makes businesses thrive. This is why we do what we do.

With that in mind, I asked our chief financial officer to create a model to understand how revenue translates to lives impacted based on our licensing agreements and client engagements. The numbers were eye-opening. By our calculations, reaching 250% growth meant that we would directly impact five million lives. *Five million people* experiencing the power of the Results Equation that fuels fulfillment, accountability, and results.

This was the clarity we needed. Our new R2 Vision was to *impact 5 million lives in 2025*. It was no longer just a financial target—it was meaningful. Every dollar earned wasn't just revenue; it was another life changed. Every workshop delivered, every leader coached, every organization transformed brought us closer to that goal.

That shift changed everything. Our team became more energized. Our clients became more engaged. And I started doing something I had never done before—I began thanking the CEOs I met with for helping us achieve our vision. Now, when I talked to CEOs, I didn't just talk to them about our services—I thanked them. I told them that by working with us, they were helping us achieve our vision of impacting five million lives. That changed the conversation. It inspired them. It made them feel like they were part of something bigger than just another vendor engagement.

This is the power of a great vision. It rallies people. It makes your organization magnetic. And it aligns with your purpose.

To craft an effective vision—your R2—it must pass the 3M test:

1. **Meaningful**—It should inspire. People should feel connected to it and believe in it. This is the "so what" test: If we achieve this vision, what impact will it have?
2. **Measurable**—You must be able to track progress toward your vision. Without measurement, it's just a wish.
3. **Memorable**—If no one in your organization remembers it, it's useless. A strong vision should be simple, clear, and easy to recall, just like your purpose. Simple scales.

To create your R2 Vision statement, start by imagining that it is three to five years from now. Your organization has achieved something incredible—something that transformed the way you operate, serve your customers, and impact the world. You're leaving your role, and the person who comes next reflects on your accomplishment and thinks, *Wow, that leader left a legacy of execution.*

What does that look like? That's your starting point.

Defining it isn't enough. To create real momentum, your vision needs to pass the 3M test: Is it meaningful? Is it measurable? Is it memorable?

Then, connect it back to your purpose. Your entire Results Equation is one core narrative. Each element needs to fit and be connected to the previous element. Make sure your vision aligns with your purpose.

We worked with a state prison system responsible for more than thirty correctional facilities that was facing a host of problems: severe understaffing, inconsistent facility management, and low morale among officers. Recruitment and retention numbers showed these problems. Turnover among correctional officers had reached 39%, with some facilities operating with vacancy rates exceeding 50%. When we ended up working with this prison system, we started with their Results Equation. The most significant alignment was around their R2 Vision—to be officially recognized as a Great Place to Work. This was a profound vision that made clear that this wasn't just about reducing turnover or improving efficiency—it was about transforming the entire experience of working there. It sent a bold message: We don't just want to be better than we were yesterday; we want to be the kind of place where people are proud to work.

We will revisit this story in more detail in the alignment section, but after just one year of working with us, their turnover dropped from 39% to 30%. The following year: 26%. They are well on their way to achieving their vision.

Remember, in creating your R2 Vision, you are laying the foundation for a profound experience that will shape the beliefs of your employees and your customers. The statement *is* an experience that will drive beliefs about who you are as an organization. Ask yourself, what beliefs do I want this team to hold about us as a company and where we're headed?

This is more than a leadership exercise—it is the foundation of how your organization will think and act every day. Your R2 Vision isn't just a target; it's a declaration of who you are and where you're going. When it's done right, it becomes the heartbeat of your culture, shaping behaviors, decisions, and ultimately, results.

CHAPTER 7

KEY RESULTS

When we began our relationship with Brinker International, a leading casual dining company known for its iconic brands like Chili's Grill & Bar, Brinker operated more than 1,600 locations in twenty-nine countries. The company had a passion for culture. We've been with them so long they were featured in almost every book we've published, from *The Oz Principle* in 1994 to *Change the Culture, Change the Game* in 2012.

One story that hasn't been told was when one of our founders, Tom Smith, was meeting with the executive team to discuss putting together their Key Results. He asked the team what they wanted to achieve, and they all agreed that profit margin was a top priority. He asked them if they had aligned around a Key Result for profit margin, and they nodded their heads.

One leader confidently said, "Yes, 3 percent." Another chimed in, "No, it's 5 percent." Then a third executive, equally assured, said, "Seven percent."

A moment of silence had them all turning to the CEO for clarity. The CEO leaned back and said, "Well, the goal is somewhere between 3 and 7 percent." Everyone in the room chuckled, realizing a key problem. If we're not clear in this room, how can we expect our employees to be clear across 1,600 locations?

And they're not alone. We see this all the time, so we decided to take a deeper look at this issue as part of our executive alignment sessions. We studied more than a hundred companies that came to us looking to drive alignment. But before we could help them align, we needed to ask a critical question: Alignment toward what?

When we assessed those one hundred companies, we found that only twenty-four of them had a leadership team that had clarity on the Key Results. That means in 76% of cases, leaders were pushing their teams toward different targets without even realizing it. And if the leaders weren't clear, how could alignment possibly scale across an entire organization?

This lack of clarity isn't just a leadership issue—it cascades throughout the company, leading to misaligned priorities, wasted efforts, and employees working toward different versions of success. It's no wonder so many businesses struggle with execution.

This can happen for many reasons. Sometimes, the leaders have different numbers in their heads, but they're all correct—3 percent was what they told the markets, 5 percent was what they told employees, and 7 percent was their stretch goal. These variations on the target exist across industries. But when different parts of the organization are operating with different definitions of success, execution becomes scattered, and results suffer.

For other organizations, the problem is complexity.

Such was the case with a healthcare company we worked with that was headquartered in St. Petersburg, Florida, and had about 30,000 employees. In our first meeting, after the typical round of introductions, the CEO launched into the heart of the matter.

"We need more accountability," he said. "We're not delivering our results. Patient satisfaction is down, and our operating costs are up."

We pressed him to say more about the lack of accountability and what he wanted to achieve by addressing it. "We are crystal clear on what we're trying to achieve around here," he said. "I send our goals out every week to my team in an email."

This caught us off guard. We don't hear this very often, and we took it as a good sign.

The CEO pulled out a folder from his desk. In it, he had a list of 124 different Key Results. This is what he sends around weekly. At this point, we knew what we were dealing with. The CEO's intentions were sound, of course, but 124 Key Results? How could they all possibly be key? And who would ever read them all?

Imagine receiving a weekly email from the CEO with 124 goals to work toward. Where would you start? We wouldn't blame you if you stopped opening the email. Or perhaps you open the email and scan the list for the few metrics that are most relevant to your job, ignoring the rest. This drives a silo mentality.

What you need instead is a few results that are relevant to everybody across the entire organization. This is where psychologists Edwin Locke and Gary Latham's famous Goal Setting Theory becomes especially relevant.[13] Their decades of research in organizational psychology show that setting specific and challenging goals, combined with commitment, feedback, and attention to task complexity, leads to higher performance. In other words, when goals are clear, meaningful, and measurable, people are more likely to stay motivated and aligned. Applying this framework at scale—across thousands of employees—ensures not just direction but also drive.

Brinker International recognized this opportunity. They didn't just talk about culture—they made it a strategic priority. By creating clarity, they were able to drive alignment at every level of the organization, empowering their teams to execute with confidence. They not only achieved their R2 after working with us, but they went on to set and smash an R3 and have now moved on to their R4.

Brinker is a shining example of how companies can build a culture that drives results—not just once, but always. Their journey proves that true transformation starts with clarity, and when leaders are aligned, the entire organization can get aligned (more on alignment in the next section).

Remember, Key Results sit within the larger context of your Results Equation. They are the measurable milestones that indicate whether you are on track to achieve your R2 Vision. If your vision is the mountain peak, Key Results are the trail markers keeping you on the right path.

Every organization, every department, and every individual should have their own Key Results. They cascade from the top, ensuring that everyone is rowing in the same direction. But they must follow the 3M framework to be effective.

Meaningful

Like the R2 Vision, the Key Results must be meaningful. But unlike the R2 Vision, they don't need to inspire as powerfully. In our experience, most company-wide Key Results fall into one of four categories:

Financial Key Results

Financial Key Results are the most common and easiest to measure. They include revenue growth, profit margin, EBITDA, stock price, and cost reduction. These are the numbers that executives report to shareholders, boards, and investors.

Operational Key Results

Operational Key Results measure how efficiently the business runs. These include metrics like speed to market, supply chain efficiency, production output, and quality control. Sometimes Key Results can be in the form of completing a project. To launch a website or finish a project by a deadline can also be considered a measurable Key Result. One hundred percent completion is the measurement.

Customer-Focused Key Results

Customer-focused Key Results reflect how well a company is serving its market. They include metrics such as Net Promoter Score (NPS), customer retention, satisfaction ratings, and market share.

People Key Results

People Key Results focus on the workforce—employee engagement, turnover rates, employee NPS scores, or achieving goals such as Great Place to Work achievements.

Memorable

Key Results need to be simple and clear enough for people to remember. The Rule of Three is powerful—people can recall three priorities. More than three, it won't scale, and you risk losing people's attention and weakening the impact you're after. It must be clear and memorable from employee number one to employee number 100,000 and everyone in between. People retain information in threes. The Rule of Three, as it's known, has been proven by cognitive psychologists[14] and practiced by speechwriters and ad copywriters, who came up with such slogans as Just Do It! and Snap! Crackle! Pop![15]

A manufacturing company we worked with had a senior VP who swore her division needed six Key Results. She insisted, "They're all equally important!" After some back-and-forth, we asked, "If you could only focus on three today—just today—which would they be?"

She paused, thought for a moment, and then the clarity hit her. "These three."

That's the breakthrough moment we aim for. When you force prioritization, you simplify and create clarity. Simplicity drives memorability, and what's memorable can scale.

Measurable

To be measurable you need to be able to track progress with a clear metric. And importantly, you must identify the target! For example, "Improve client NPS" is not a Key Result. "Improve client NPS to 75" is a Key Result. The following are some Key Results across a wide range of industries that we have gathered over the years:

- Financial: $863 million in net sales
- Financial: Deliver margin of $0.48 per pound

- Financial: Grow faster than market average
- Financial: 10% return on equity
- Operational: Number-one pizza of choice
- Operational: Ten acquisitions
- Operational: 30% reduction in cycle time
- Operational: 25% of total sales from new products
- Customer-Focused: Patient satisfaction of 4.7
- Customer Focused: JD Power score of 700
- Customer-Focused: One million clients
- Customer-Focused: Products per member from 1.98 to 2.2
- People: 70% employee engagement
- People: Maximum 10% employee turnover
- People: 74% inclusion score
- People: Safety goal of zero recordables

The Key Result Litmus Test

Key Results must align seamlessly with every element of your Results Equation—they aren't just isolated targets; they are the stepping stones to your R2 Vision. If your R2 is a three- or five-year vision, your Key Results must be laser-focused on what needs to happen this year to keep you on track.

Each year, you should reset, refine, and reinforce your Key Results to ensure continuous progress toward your ultimate goal. The Key Results must also align with your purpose. If we achieve these Key Results this year, will we have been aligned with our why?

In the next chapter, we'll dive into the next critical element of the Results Equation: Strategic Drivers. While Key Results define what success looks like, Strategic Drivers determine how you'll get there. These are the focused initiatives, big bets, and operational priorities that will move the needle toward achieving your Key Results. It is critical that your Strategic Drivers are tightly aligned with your Key Results. We'll explore how to identify, prioritize, and reinforce the right Strategic Drivers to ensure that every action in your organization is propelling you toward your R2 Vision. When you get Key Results right, you create clarity—and clear is kind.

CHAPTER 8

STRATEGIC DRIVERS

In a world where higher education is facing disruption from every angle—declining enrollment, rising tuition, AI-driven learning models, and shifting workforce demands—twenty-five academic deans from institutions across the country gathered in one room, not as competitors but as collaborators. They weren't just focused on their own schools' survival; they were thinking bigger. They were asking: *What does the future of higher education look like? And how do we ensure that we are ready for it?*

This was before my (Jessica's) time at Culture Partners, when I was a sole consultant, facilitating leadership retreats for a variety of clients. I began the day with a meditation in which I asked the group to imagine twenty years from now. What has happened at a macro level? What possible futures might emerge? Then we went around and shared our ideas until we had collected one hundred distinct possibilities. No idea was too big and no scenario too wild. The more divergent the possibilities, the more valuable the exercise.

Of course, AI was on the list along with global pandemics, but some ideas surprised me. Full banking system collapse appeared on the list as well as first alien contact and unlimited clean energy.

From these one hundred futures, I had the deans vote on the most critical dynamics—the ones that would have the biggest impact on the trajectory of higher education. Once identified, we mapped them onto a spectrum of reality.

For example, for geopolitical stability, one extreme was world peace while the other was global warfare. For technological advancement, one extreme was a world where AI replaces teachers entirely, while the other was a technological plateau where traditional teaching remains dominant.

Then, I asked them to pair two completely different critical dynamics and place them on an X and Y axis to explore four possible future worlds. Let's take two examples: climate change severity (minimal vs. extreme) and AI's role in education (minimal vs. dominant). For each resulting world, they had to identify the appropriate strategy.

1. **World 1: The AI Renaissance**
   (Minimal Climate Change, Dominant AI)
   - AI-driven learning eliminates the need for human professors. Universities become certification hubs rather than knowledge centers. The need for physical campuses declines as students learn from AI tutors.
   - *Strategy:* Invest heavily in AI integration and develop partnerships with leading AI research firms to stay competitive.

2. **World 2: The Sustainable Campus**
   (Extreme Climate Change, Minimal AI)
   - Climate refugees drive a mass migration of students, forcing universities to rethink their physical infrastructure. Sustainability becomes the number one priority. AI remains a minor tool, with human faculty leading learning.
   - *Strategy:* Universities pivot to building self-sustaining campuses with renewable energy and water solutions.

3. **World 3: The Hybrid Academy**
   (Minimal Climate Change, Minimal AI)
   - Traditional education remains largely intact, but with incremental changes. Institutions struggle to attract students as alternatives (bootcamps, online certifications) grow in popularity.
   - *Strategy:* Focus on unique value propositions such as experiential learning and global study programs to maintain relevance.

4. **World 4: The Virtual University**
   (Extreme Climate Change, Dominant AI)
   - Campuses are abandoned due to climate disasters. AI becomes the primary educational tool. Universities exist only as virtual institutions.
   - *Strategy:* Invest in digital infrastructure, VR-based classrooms, and global student recruitment.

At this point, the exercise shifted from exploring wild possibilities to something more grounded, what people believed was most likely. Because what we believe about the future shapes how we prepare for it. And preparation isn't just about reacting to trends; it's about influencing them.

So, I pushed the deans further. What beliefs did they hold about the future of higher education? What about their faculty, their students, their boards? If they assumed AI would take over, were they passively accepting it as inevitable or actively shaping how AI would integrate into learning? If they believed higher education was in decline, were they unknowingly creating that reality through hesitation and fear-driven decision-making?

Next, we examined experiences. Because beliefs don't form in a vacuum—they're shaped by what people see, hear, and feel. I asked: What experiences would indicate that higher education was heading in a particular direction? What would signal, beyond a doubt, that a seismic shift was underway? A Fortune 500 company dropping degree requirements? (That has already begun.) A major university shutting down permanently?

Then came the final, and most important, question: What experiences could they create to drive the right beliefs within their teams? If they wanted faculty to embrace AI rather than resist it, what experience would make them believe AI was a tool rather than a threat? If they wanted students to see a college degree as valuable despite the rise of alternative credentials, what kind of immersive, transformational learning experience would prove it to them?

We did this exercise with four other X and Y charts, identifying twenty possible future realities that we could prepare for.

In the end, the deans realized that their job wasn't just to react to the future—it was to shape it. They weren't just observers of higher education's fate; they were architects of it. And the most powerful tool they had wasn't policy or curriculum—it was the ability to create experiences that shaped beliefs, which in turn drove action.

And that's when I saw the shift in the room. The conversation moved from fear of what might happen to accountability for what could be built. This was a robust strategic exercise. It didn't just help institutions prepare for the future—it aligned leadership teams in their way of thinking. It forced them to break free from the Action Trap, where leaders often react to immediate challenges rather than preparing for long-term change.

That exercise was an ideal scenario for strategic planning, a level of scenario planning that most corporations never engage in. How many Fortune 500 executive teams are willing to put two entire workdays into this type of thinking? You would be hard pressed to get more than a few hours.

Instead, what we typically see is the opposite: leadership teams trapped in reactionary cycles, making decisions based on short-term pressures rather than a long-term vision. Or in the worst case, CEOs who dictate the future from the top down, convinced they already have the answers. This is the command-and-control approach. Leaders exacting their will on an organization, coming from a place of ego because ultimately, they are making decisions from a place of fear. These strategies rarely sing.

The most common approach to strategy development looks like a leadership team spending an afternoon in a conference room scribbling ideas on sticky notes, voting on the most popular ones, and calling it a strategy. Employees—those closest to the work, who live the company's challenges—are completely left out of the process. The result? Initiatives that fail to gain traction, cultures built on compliance rather than commitment, and organizations that find themselves blindsided by disruption instead of prepared for it. Down the line, leaders complain that their teams lack accountability.

The best strategies involve a process in which leaders elevate the voices of employees and uncover what strategies are most relevant. Through focus groups, interviews, and surveys, humble leaders ask employees: What are the biggest strategic priorities? What challenges do you see coming? What opportunities should we pursue?

Asking questions is an underrated leadership skill. Many executives assume they already have the answers. But strategy is most powerful when it emerges from a combination of leadership insight and on-the-ground experience. Own that you don't know it all, ask colleagues for input, and great things can happen. Leaders don't have to have all the answers, but they can set the conditions for the best answers to emerge and then make a decision.

For Strategic Drivers to be effective, they must align with Key Results and R2 Vision. Another way to think about Strategic Drivers is to ask, "What will have the greatest impact on achieving our R2 Vision?" They are not isolated priorities—they are part of a larger system. If strategy isn't tied to measurable outcomes, it becomes abstract, vague, and ineffective.

For example, we've seen the following Strategic Drivers succeed in these industries:

- **Healthcare:** *Patient-Centered Digital Innovation*—using technology to improve patient experience and outcomes.
- **Retail:** *Hyperpersonalized Customer Journeys*—leveraging AI and data to tailor experiences.

- **Financial Services:** *Radical Transparency in Banking*—building trust by being up front about fees and financial risks.
- **Higher Education:** *Skills over Degrees*—shifting to competency-based learning to align with workforce needs.
- **Technology:** *AI as a Copilot*—embedding AI into workflows to accelerate outcomes.

What do all of these successful Strategic Drivers have in common? They are simple, bold, and distinct. Because when strategy is simple, it becomes scalable. It's not just a statement on a slide—it becomes a lens through which everyone makes decisions.

Other Strategic Drivers we have seen include a focus on business automation, growth through acquisitions, launching new products, developing new capabilities, re-allocating operational expenses, embracing environmental, social, and governance principles in the organization, or delivering value-added services to the market. And while these all sound wonderful, just like Key Results, you have to focus on three.

Why? Because simplicity scales. It's how decision-making scales, empowering your teams and people to make decisions every day aligned to your three Strategic Drivers. Complexity might feel strategic, but simplicity is what drives real-world execution. When strategy is simple, it becomes repeatable, understandable, and executable across an entire organization. More than three, and execution fails to scale. People don't know what to prioritize. Resources get spread too thin. Leadership sends mixed signals. And when everything is a priority, nothing is.

But most importantly, your Strategic Drivers must align with the entire Results Equation. Remember the Stanford research—companies that had purpose, strategy, and culture aligned saw 4X growth than those that were misaligned. And strategy is constantly changing. It is not unusual for companies to shift Strategic Drivers before the end of the year to respond to the rapid pace of change. This requires not just a strategic shift but a realignment of all elements of your Results Equation alongside it. This Results Equation breathes day in and day out. As culture changes, so too does strategy, and vice versa if you want to drive results. This is adaptive alignment, another driver of growth according to the Stanford research.

A strong Strategic Driver aligns seamlessly with the Results Equation: It connects to purpose (why the company exists). It leads to R2 Vision (the finish line). It translates into Key Results (how success is measured). And it is reinforced by culture (the way people think and act to achieve results). You cannot think of one without considering the others if you want to stay in alignment.

At the heart of every great strategy is a choice: react to the future or take accountability for shaping it. This requires a shift in thinking. Surrender and stop fighting reality, have faith in the team's collective intelligence, identify what you can control, free yourself from fear, and take the next right action.

But even the most inspiring strategy won't move the needle if it's not clear and simple enough to live in people's daily decisions. Simplicity is strategic. It's not about dumbing things down—it's about sharpening your point of view so clearly that it becomes a guide for action rather than just a statement on paper.

CHAPTER 9

CULTURAL BELIEFS

It was one of those meetings where you could feel the tension before anyone spoke. The executive team of a midsize retail company had gathered for our first session. We had been brought in to help drive results after a year of sluggish growth.

Their CEO, a sharp, performance-driven leader, kicked things off: "We need to move faster. Our execution is slow. Moving forward, we need to focus on speed and urgency. What can you do to get people focused and accountable?"

Our senior partner in the room asked a simple question: "What's stopping your people from moving faster?"

Silence. Then, after a beat, the COO spoke up: "Honestly? I think they're afraid of making mistakes. They don't want to get blamed if something goes wrong."

That was the real problem. Not their strategy. Not their competency. It was the shared beliefs held by the employees. Whatever experiences they had had to date led them to the belief that risk was to be avoided and so slow was sound. Taking risks was dangerous, so they played it safe. And no amount of new strategy was going to change that belief.

This was an Action Trap in motion—executives jumping straight to action without addressing the underlying beliefs that were shaping those actions in the first place.

And they're not alone. This isn't just theory—it's backed by data. McKinsey has studied organizational health for over two decades, analyzing more than 1,500 companies across one hundred countries.[16] Their findings are clear: Companies that invest in cultural health—clarifying shared beliefs and aligning them with strategy—outperform their peers by a wide margin. One study found that organizations that improved their health saw an 18% increase in EBITDA in just one year. In major transformations, those that embedded culture into their change efforts delivered 35% higher shareholder returns than those that didn't. And during times of crisis, like the COVID-19 pandemic, companies with strong cultural health were 59% less likely to show financial distress.

We've seen this firsthand in our work with Southwest Airlines, a company that's long been known for its legendary culture. When customer satisfaction scores began to dip, they didn't just roll out a new strategy. They went to the root—empowering frontline employees with access to real-time data and reinforcing the belief that "you are the experience." This wasn't a one-off initiative. It was a belief shift, deeply embedded into their operating model. As a result, customer satisfaction rose, call handle times decreased, and the culture became even more resilient. That's the power of shaping belief to drive behavior—and behavior to drive results.

And that's where the magic happens.

The Results Equation aligns purpose, strategy, and culture to achieve results, but too many leaders make the mistake of thinking culture is a "nice-to-have" rather than the invisible force that determines whether strategy succeeds or fails.

Culture is the way that people think and act to get results. Most organizations spend a lot of time focused on the "act" part of that sentence. Far fewer spend time focusing on how people *think*.

If you're not getting the results you want, you need to ask your team two of the most powerful questions in our playbook:

1. What commonly held beliefs does the team hold today that are getting in the way of us achieving our goal?
2. And what do we want those beliefs to be?

This exercise is what we call the C1 to C2 shift exercise. It is the most important tool in your arsenal because it focuses on a shift in thinking. But here you are thinking about a collective shift, not just a personal one. This is culture. How do you, collectively, need to shift your shared beliefs in order to drive results toward your R2 Vision? This is the final element of the Results Equation and, perhaps, the most powerful.

It starts with clarity. First, collectively, pick the three Cultural Beliefs that will drive the right actions (aligned with your strategy) to get your Key Results. These should be simple, unmistakable, and directly tied to your goals. No jargon, no fluff—just the core beliefs that will drive the behaviors you need.

Then clarify even further. Each belief needs a short, powerful phrase—a two-word tagline that captures its essence. Culture thrives on repetition, simplicity, and clarity, and a memorable phrase helps people internalize the shift.

Finally, bring it to life with even more clarity—make it personal. For each belief, define a behavior in the first person, starting with "I." This turns an abstract idea into a daily practice, something people can own and embody.

For example, if the goal is collaboration, the belief might be One Team. The tagline makes it memorable, and the behavior makes it actionable: "I shatter silos and act as one." If customer focus is the priority, the belief could be Member Obsessed, with the behavior: "I deliver world-class value to our members every time."

Some other examples to get your juices flowing:

Speak Up
I seek and provide timely feedback to improve myself and our results.

Drive Trust
I lead with integrity, embrace diversity, and assume positive intent of others.

Zoom!
I learn fast, move fast, and deliver.

These aren't just phrases on a wall. They are explicit commitments to behavior. And behavior, not words, is what changes culture. Your behaviors are other people's experiences. This is when the Results Equation kicks into high gear.

Do not confuse Cultural Beliefs with values. They are different. Values are timeless. They rarely change. Cultural Beliefs are timely. They zero in on the exact beliefs your people need right now to take the actions that will power today's Strategic Drivers and deliver your Key Results.

As your strategy shifts, your Cultural Beliefs must shift too.

Review them often. Update them without hesitation. At Culture Partners, we change at least one every year—sometimes more—because staying relevant is the only way to keep your culture aligned and your results on track.

At this point, you should notice a pattern. The Results Equation mirrors the order of the Results Pyramid. Results sit at the top. Strategic Drivers (actions) sit beneath them. And beneath that, the foundation: beliefs created by experiences.

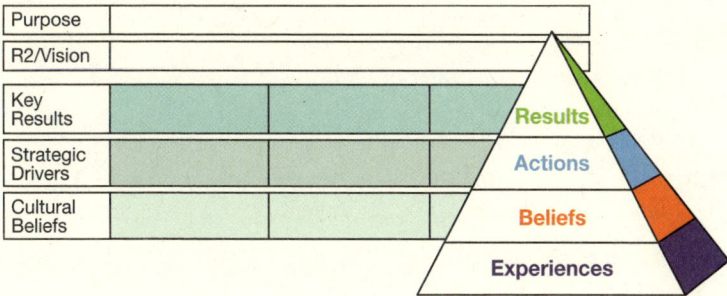

Strategy without the right beliefs is like an engine without fuel—it won't take you anywhere.

Once you have completed this step, you have your Results Equation. This will provide clarity to your organization on who you are as a company, why you exist, how you will win, and the way you will win together. One philosopher said that culture is the story we tell about who we are. This Results Equation is your story on a platter.

The next section in this book is alignment. We don't mean alignment as in more meetings or better communication. Alignment is all about focusing on experiences, the foundation of the Results Pyramid. Up to this point, all you have done is memorialize your Results Equation. Now you need to operationalize it. That is step two in unlocking your potential. Read on to learn how.

PART TWO

ALIGNMENT

CHAPTER 10

CHIEF REPETITION OFFICER

I (Joe) begin every meeting by stating our Results Equation:

> Our purpose is to drive results by activating your culture.
> If we are successful, we will be able to impact five million
> lives in 2025. Our three Key Results are $X in bookings, $X
> in EBITDA, and X% client retention. Our Strategic Drivers
> are demand generation, the subscription model, and our
> culture. And our Cultural Beliefs are Sprint Together (I act
> with urgency), Own the Outcomes (I drive client results),
> and Solve Creatively (I adapt to grow).

Such repetition doesn't come easily. One day, I had three
meetings in a row. First, an executive team meeting where I opened
with the same grounding statement. Then a sales team huddle
where I repeated it again. And finally, an all-hands meeting where,
once more, I reinforced the message. By the end of the day, I was

feeling, frankly, ridiculous.

I started to feel like a robot and feared I was starting to insult the team by repeating the Results Equation every time. I didn't want to come across as pedantic. Then one of my executives sent me this email:

> Joe, I want to recognize you for how you really own the outcomes. I appreciate how you ground us in who we are every single time we start a meeting. I thought by the third call today that you might not repeat our Results Equation, but when you did, it showed the team that you really believe in our work and are committed to this team and who we are. By doing that, you are going to positively impact our ability to impact five million lives in 2025.

That's when it hit me. Feeling ridiculous? That was my ego talking. The repetition wasn't about me—it was about creating

alignment so deeply in the team that it became second nature. It wasn't about making speeches or belittling the team; it was about demonstrating accountability for our Results Equation to create alignment. Ultimately, it's about creating an experience for the team that drives the right belief.

A well-known fact about leadership is that alignment is hard. People don't absorb a message the first time, or even the fifth time. It takes repetition, consistency, and an unwavering commitment. And that takes swallowing my pride and embracing my secondary role as CRO (chief repetition officer).

This requires a shift in thinking.

- **Stop fighting reality**—An email plus a town hall is not enough to embed our Results Equations into this organization. And it's not enough for yours.
- **Have faith**—If our team is clear on our Results Equation, they will be able to achieve things in ways I couldn't possibly imagine.
- **Identify what's yours**—I am accountable for aligning the team, and I can do that by repeating it every time we meet.
- **Free yourself from fear**—So what if I think I look ridiculous? This isn't about me. It's about them. And, as my colleague told me via email, it's not silly. It's purposeful.
- **Take the next right action**—Commit to creating a consistent experience: Become the chief repetition officer.

We all understand the importance of exercise, yet so few of us commit to a routine. We all know that gym memberships spike in January, only for attendance to drop off steadily in February and March. The same principle—you've got to show up if you want to get in shape—applies to organizational culture. It becomes who you are. As with diet and exercise, it's all about consistency. If you don't maintain momentum, your culture will falter and your results will suffer.

Andy Jassy, CEO of Amazon, put it plainly: "Keeping your culture strong is not a birthright. You have to work at it all the time . . . ."[17] You don't set it once and expect it to stick. It requires ongoing effort and commitment. And if you, as a leader, aren't diligently reinforcing it, then who will? This is a key part of any leader's job.

One tech CEO we worked with described it best: "Unless I consciously manage the culture, like my golf swing, muscle memory takes over and I'm back to my old ways. Culture has a powerful memory. We need to create new memories."

The key to creating those new memories? Repetition.

The power of repetition leads to greater understanding of your why, your how, and your way. A few years ago, we worked with a restaurant chain that had set a bold financial goal: a 5% profit margin across all locations. A difficult target in the food industry. The leadership team knew that to achieve it, everyone—down to the waitstaff—needed to understand how their individual actions impacted the business. So, they started each shift with a five-minute "heart-of-the-house huddle," and it started with reciting the Results Equation.

At the beginning of the huddles, the managers would ask, "How do you impact profit margin?" At first, the waitstaff shrugged. "I clean tables." But after weeks of repetition, the answers began to change. "The faster I clean tables, the more guests we can seat. The more guests we serve, the more money we make. The more money we make, the better our profit margin."

They got it. And once they got it, they started acting on it. That is the power of surrender. They rolled out the process and trusted that the results would follow.

To embed alignment into your organization, you need a clear, repeatable way to talk about your Results Equation. Imagine it like a run-on sentence.

It's simple:

Our purpose is to (purpose statement).

If we are successful, we will (insert R2 Vision).

We will measure success this year by (insert Key Results).

Our Strategic Drivers to achieve those results are (insert Strategic Drivers).

And the way we do this is (insert Cultural Beliefs).

Here's an example from Suncoast Credit Union:

Our purpose is to improve the financial lives of our members, and if we are successful, we will reach 2.5 million members by 2030. This year we will achieve 11% in annual member growth, a net promoter score of 80, and an app rating of 4.8. These are our Key Results towards the Strategic Drivers of growth through price and financial wellness, to be the member's advocate and to be envied in digital delivery. The way we'll do this is through our Cultural Beliefs of Got It, Do It, Grow It.

This isn't about turning people into corporate robots. It's about creating an experience of clarity so that people can make decisions with confidence, knowing exactly what the company stands for and how their role contributes to its success.

You might think your team has heard it enough. They haven't. You might feel like you're repeating yourself. You are. That's the point. You might worry that you sound like a broken record. Good. Because that's how alignment happens.

When we coach leaders, we tell them to start every meeting—yes, *every* meeting—with their Results Equation. Just as we do at Culture Partners. Whether it's an all-hands meeting or a quick one-on-one, it doesn't matter. The repetition creates clarity. Clarity creates alignment. And alignment drives results. One note: Repetition doesn't mean it becomes rote. That is always a risk—and if your team doesn't believe you believe what you're saying, you will know it.

One CEO we worked with took this to heart and incorporated the Results Equation into every conversation. His team at first used to roll their eyes. But a few months in, something shifted. People started taking turns repeating the Results Equation, and managers deep in the organization could recite it by heart. How many of your middle managers know your purpose statement by heart? What about your vision? Your Key Results? I'm guessing not many.

"Repetition is the mother of all learning." So, here's the challenge: Take it on. Own the role of chief repetition officer. Start your meetings with the Results Equation. Reinforce it every chance you get. When your people can see themselves in the vision, they bring it to life. And that's how you reach your full potential.

CHAPTER 11

FOCUSED
RECOGNITION

When my (Jessica's) daughter Eleanor took her first steps, I remember how amazed I was that this tiny thing came out of my belly and was now mobile. After a couple adorable steps, she stumbled and fell onto the carpet. The room exploded with noise. The whole family was there, and we were all beaming. "Oh, my goodness, Ellie! We're so proud of you! Do it again, do it again!"

And what exactly were we cheering for? Was it the flawless stride? The perfect heel-to-toe form? No. We were celebrating the step—however wobbly—and completely ignoring that she plopped onto her butt after two, maybe three steps max. When we said to do "it" again, we were referring to the step, not the fall.

What we didn't say was, "Ellie, let's talk about that fall. Have you considered adjusting your center of gravity?" We weren't giving her gait feedback or rating her ankle flexibility on a five-point scale. We were just thrilled she was moving forward.

And yet, in corporate America, we do the opposite. We spend so much time giving feedback on the fall that we forget to cheer for the step. We pounce on missed deadlines, failed launches, or messy presentations—but barely pause when someone nails it.

So, let's talk about what it looks like when we really start cheering for the steps.

As we mentioned in chapter five, we once worked with a state prison system responsible for more than thirty correctional facilities that was facing a host of problems: severe understaffing, inconsistent facility management, and low morale among officers. The situation had deteriorated to the point where, in some prisons, the inmates were effectively running the facilities. As you can imagine, this led to an increase in violence. These are not your typical office jobs.

The challenges of staffing shortages and workplace safety concerns were compounded by public perception. The prison system struggled with a negative reputation in the media, where reports of contraband smuggling, staff misconduct, and unsafe working conditions contributed to hiring difficulties. Additionally, law enforcement agencies across the nation were facing challenges postpandemic, adding to the recruitment challenges.

Recruitment and retention numbers showed these problems. Turnover among correctional officers had reached 39%, with some facilities operating with vacancy rates exceeding 50%, making it clear that major cultural shifts were necessary to address systemic challenges.

When a new commissioner took over in 2023, he recognized the need for a cultural overhaul. Instead of viewing the department's problems solely through the lens of operational inefficiencies, he saw that a shift in workplace culture—focused on clarity, alignment, and accountability—could lead to real change.

When we ended up working with this prison system, we started with their Results Equation. The most significant alignment was around their R2 Vision—to be officially recognized as a Great Place to Work. This was a profound vision that made clear that this wasn't just about reducing turnover or improving efficiency—it was about transforming the entire experience of working there. It sent a bold message: We don't just want to be better than we were yesterday; we want to be the kind of place where people are proud to work.

That vision might have seemed impossible given their starting point, but that's exactly why it mattered. It was a radical departure from the status quo, signaling to employees that leadership wasn't just tinkering around the edges. They were committed to real change.

To get there, we needed to create alignment around the Cultural Beliefs that would drive this transformation. One of the biggest gaps? Recognition.

Officers only heard about their performance when they messed up. Leadership had inherited a long-standing culture of, fittingly, correction. They had systems in place to track failures, discipline mistakes, and document every policy infraction—but no structured way to recognize positive contributions. In fact, they had a literal Wall of Shame. In many facilities, wardens listed officers who had been disciplined or terminated on the Wall for public shaming. While the intent may have been to encourage better behavior, the result was anything but: A culture of fear and negativity took hold.

We recommended an immediate shift: removing the Wall of Shame and replacing it with a Wall of Fame, where leadership would publicly acknowledge officers who demonstrated positive behaviors. Some facilities adopted focused recognition cards to highlight behaviors aligned with the department's new Cultural Beliefs. Officers could now receive written recognition for actions demonstrating collaboration, innovation, or ownership.

Additionally, leaders were trained to integrate focused recognition into daily routines, ensuring that cultural transformation wasn't confined to occasional meetings but became part of everyday operations. Employees were encouraged to acknowledge each other's efforts, reinforcing a more positive and engaged workforce. They committed to providing focused recognition to their peers twice a week.

The impact of recognition on workplace performance is well documented. In corporate settings, organizations that focus on celebrating desired behaviors—rather than punishing failures—see higher engagement, stronger performance, and lower turnover. The same applied at this prison system: When officers felt valued, they were more likely to stay engaged, reducing the staffing crisis.

And it worked.

After one year, turnover dropped from 39% to 30%. The following year: 26%. One leader told us, "I've received more recognition in the past three months than I did in the previous three decades."

That's not a throwaway line. That's a culture shift.

And the impact showed up where it mattered most: safety.

When officers felt valued and supported, they weren't just more likely to stay—they were more likely to stay engaged. That shift in engagement led to better decision-making, stronger teamwork, and a more proactive approach to managing high-risk situations.

The result? A 10% reduction in safety incidents department-wide, with some facilities seeing even greater results. Two transitional centers reduced incidents by over 30%, and two state prisons reduced incidents by over 40%.

That's not a coincidence. When people feel seen for doing the right thing, they do more of it. Recognition reinforced the behaviors that kept officers and inmates safer, creating a ripple effect that improved the overall stability of the facilities.

And all of this started with a simple shift—from focusing on failure to celebrating progress.

This wasn't a onetime initiative—it was a fundamental shift in how the organization operated. Recognition became part of the culture, not just an afterthought. And that recognition led to alignment around the Cultural Beliefs they needed to shift in order to drive the right action to achieve their Key Results.

This state prison's transformation is ongoing, but the department's ultimate goal—to be officially recognized as a Great Place to Work—would have seemed impossible just a few years ago. Today, it stands as an ambitious yet achievable vision.

Why? Because recognition is more than a thank-you. It's a belief-shifter. It's an experience that says: I see you. I see what you're doing. And it matters.

Putting Focused Recognition into Practice

Recognition is positive, but it needs to be done well. A Slack channel called #kudos will not transform your culture.

Let's start with what recognition doesn't look like. It doesn't look like half-hearted emails that say, "Good job," delivered with the enthusiasm of an HR email about open enrollment. It doesn't look like an emoji on Slack or Teams. And it definitely doesn't look like the corporate equivalent of a "like" button. In our AI-enabled world, this is becoming far too common.

For John Frehse, the AI takeover—even of small things—is

depressing. John is a labor strategy expert at a consulting firm and a good friend of ours. Every June, like clockwork, John starts dreading his work anniversary because he knows what's coming: a tsunami of AI-generated congratulations on LinkedIn.

Last year, he got seventy-five messages. Seventy-five. All of them said the exact same thing: "Congratulations on seven years with Ankura Consulting Group, LLC."

They looked the same because they were the same. Every single one of those messages, including the one from his head of corporate communications, came from people who clicked a prewritten prompt to "recognize" John's tenure.

No thought. No effort. No heart. The irony of being "seen" seventy-five times and still feeling invisible isn't lost on him. That kind of recognition isn't just ineffective—it's insulting.

John's experience is a perfect example of what can happen when recognition is an empty gesture. It's not that people don't want to acknowledge good work—it's that they're doing it in the laziest way possible. They're checking a box, not creating an experience.

Random "attaboys" and "great jobs" are fine, but they don't create alignment. The Focused Recognition tool does. The key to effective recognition is aligning the recognition to all levels of the Results Pyramid. You are recognizing someone's action. But you are not stopping there. You are tying that action to a belief and then connecting it all the way up to a Key Result or the R2 Vision. That is intentional culture creation—and how you move from cheerleading to alignment.

Here's how the Focused Recognition framework works:

I want to recognize [name] for demonstrating the Cultural Belief of [belief] in the following way [briefly describe the action]. By doing this, they positively impacted our key result of [R2 or result].

This structure transforms a kind gesture into a strategic act of clarity, alignment, and accountability. You're reinforcing what matters most in your culture by helping people connect how they behave with what the organization achieves.

At the state prison system, one of their Cultural Beliefs was Change Agent: *I promote and encourage new ways of thinking and operating.* That belief was directly tied to a Strategic Driver—Agency Innovation—which supported their Key Result: $15 million reinvested into the system.

That's not just a slogan. That's a belief fueling action that drives results.

As officers began to receive Focused Recognition for demonstrating Change Agent behaviors, it signaled that innovation wasn't just allowed—it was expected and celebrated. Over time, the cultural muscle for creativity got stronger.

Eventually, that belief system led to the launch of a full-scale Agency Innovation Program, where frontline staff were encouraged to submit ideas for improving efficiency. One of those ideas? Switching training materials from printed binders to Chromebooks.

That single idea saved the department $1.2 million annually. That savings was reinvested into opening regional training centers, which drastically improved recruitment efforts across the state.

Let's sum it up. The action was an officer suggesting a smarter, more efficient way to deliver training. The Cultural Belief was Change Agent—promoting new ways of thinking and operating. The impact was $1.2 million reinvested toward the Key Result of $15 million reinvested. And it sounds like this:

> I want to recognize Jordan for demonstrating the Cultural Belief of Change Agent.
>
> He identified an opportunity to transition training materials from printed binders to Chromebooks, reducing costs and improving accessibility for staff. By thinking differently and challenging the status quo, he showed a commitment to innovation and continuous improvement, and it saved us $1.2 million.
>
> By doing this, he directly impacted our Key Result of $15 million reinvested into the system.

That's Focused Recognition in action. And it isn't top-down. It works peer-to-peer, bottom-up, across teams, across levels. It can be a card, a comment in a meeting, a mention in a Slack or Teams channel, part of your Human Capital Management (HCM) software, or a note on someone's desk. It can be public or private, physical or digital—it just needs to be real, specific, and tied to what matters.

Focused Recognition is the tool that creates the experience to shift beliefs to align with your Cultural Belief (the shifts you need to make) to create the actions toward the results you want.

Let's go back to Eleanor for a moment. She didn't learn to walk because we critiqued her fall; she learned because we celebrated forward motion, and that consistent reinforcement gave her clarity and encouragement to try again. That's the behavior we're going for—not perfection but progress.

Your organization is on a journey of transformation—from C1 (where you are today) to C2 (where you want to be). And just like Ellie, people are going to fall. But if all you do is point out the falls, you miss the opportunity to celebrate the steps forward.

So, here's what you need to do:

1. **Make recognition visible.** Put it where people can see it—on walls, in Slack or Teams, in meetings.
2. **Make it accessible.** Don't overcomplicate it with forms or approvals. Keep it fast and easy.
3. **Make it specific.** Tie every recognition to a belief and a result.
4. **Make it constant.** Not just annual reviews. Not just big wins. Do it twice a week.

Because culture doesn't change in leaps. It changes in steps. Tiny ones. Made visible. Repeated often. Reinforced with love.

For a quick reference on best practices to implement what you've learned in this chapter, visit surrendertolead.com/resources. There you will find our Focused Recognition Best Practices Guide.

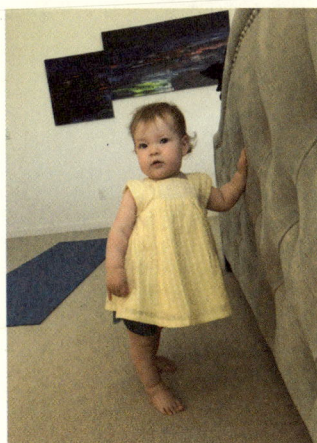

CHAPTER 12

FOCUSED STORYTELLING

When your people are aligned on the Results Equation, amazing things will happen. New behaviors emerge. People across the organization produce astounding results.

This is one such story.

Lockheed Martin found itself at a crossroads. The company's Marietta, Georgia, site, which was responsible for upgrading the Air Force's C-5 Super Galaxy aircraft, was in serious trouble. Halfway through a six-year contract, the project was $200 million over budget and failing to meet expectations.

The situation demanded technical corrections but also a cultural transformation because, as we hope you agree by now, culture is the cornerstone of driving results—even when it comes to addressing technical changes. After all, those changes happen from a team of people, and that team needs to be aligned with the overarching results you're after.

In this case, the contract was at risk, which meant so were

a lot of jobs. The Lockheed Martin site in Marietta employed about 5,000 people at the time, with roughly 1,300 working on the C-5 program. That in itself can motivate people—either to get on board with the plan to save the program or to hunt for work elsewhere.

The Marietta site was plagued by a lack of accountability, leading to inefficiency and people playing the blame game. Teams, such as the "wing team" and "fuselage team," were stuck in a cycle of finger-pointing that led to people redoing work, over and over. It was a painful pattern of inefficiency and waste. Some people naturally became bitter.

When one team handed off incomplete or faulty work, the next team would send it back instead of collaborating to fix the issue. This behavior, characterized by defensiveness and a reluctance to take ownership, was inflating costs and dragging the project further behind schedule.

Ray Burick, an engineer by trade and newly promoted to program leader, recognized the urgent need for a culture overhaul. "I knew what I was walking into," he said in an interview. He said his boss told him one thing: "Stop the bleeding."

As an engineer, Ray knows it's critical to follow processes, especially when working on aircraft. A major problem, he said, was that the organization doing the work wasn't putting the process first, and that led to disarray.

Ray identified several respected people across the organization and recruited them to work on shifting the culture. Our team worked with Ray and these champions to instill a deep sense of accountability throughout the organization.

Identifying the Key Results the organization needed to achieve wasn't hard: reduce costs, meet delivery schedules, and ensure quality. With these results in focus, the team crafted Cultural Beliefs to guide behavior. One pivotal belief was "One C-5," emphasizing that all teams were part of a unified effort rather than adversaries.

Leadership played a crucial role and took the first step. Ray and his team modeled the desired behaviors, flipping the organizational pyramid. Instead of top-down directives, leadership positioned themselves as supporters of those doing the work, creating an environment where employees felt valued and empowered. They focused on willing the good of others.

This shift is crucial. We've seen it at businesses and organizations of all sorts. When leaders shift their mindset to one of serving and empowering, creating experiences that align with their Cultural Beliefs, positive change is rapid. Command-and-control wasn't Ray's style—not by a long stretch. And it ended up that his we're-all-in-this-together approach was key.

Instead of traditional all-hands meetings, Ray held a series of town halls. These smaller, interactive sessions allowed employees to ask questions and share concerns. He committed to responding quickly to employee feedback. This is important: When you tell employees you want feedback and set an environment and process to receive it, you better act. This doesn't always happen, and, not surprisingly, that further erodes credibility at the top.

One of the most remarkable shifts was the expectation of accountability across all levels of the organization. Storytelling was at the heart of this shift. It was critical that everyone from engineers to janitors understood the goals and their responsibility in achieving them. "We started teaching everybody the entirety of the business, and how they had control of the outcome," said Ray. Employees learned about financial performance, quality metrics, and the impact of their contributions to overall results.

But he didn't just train them. He developed a way to explain the business model to every group. Ray called it the McDonald's Story—and he would compare the business to what happens when you order at a McDonald's drive-through.

The analogy was structured around the four key fundamentals of any company: Orders, Sales, EBIT (Earnings Before Interest and Taxes), and Cash. By equating Lockheed Martin's aircraft contracts to McDonald's food orders, employees could see how each stage of the process is interconnected and ultimately affects financial outcomes.

Here's the quick version of the story: Imagine a customer— represented as the US Air Force—pulling up to a McDonald's drive-through and placing an order for five Big Macs and three orders of French fries. In Lockheed Martin's case, this translates to the Air Force ordering a set number of C-5 aircraft. Like in a fast-food transaction, there is an expectation that the order will be fulfilled exactly as requested—on time, with the correct specifications, and at the agreed-upon price.

When the Air Force reaches the delivery window, they expect to receive their aircraft as promised. In return, they provide payment, much like a McDonald's customer handing over money for their meal. However, just as McDonald's does not simply pocket all the revenue but must cover costs such as employee wages, equipment, rent, and supplies, Lockheed Martin must allocate its revenue to operational costs, salaries, materials, infrastructure, and other business expenses before generating profit.

The McDonald's Story helped employees understand that revenue does not equate to immediate profit. Many workers saw large government contracts—often in the billions—and assumed the company was generating massive profit margins. But through this analogy, they learned how money flows through the business, including interest payments on loans, taxes, reinvestment into new projects, and covering day-to-day operational expenses.

The McDonald's Story was powerful and effective at starting to shift the mindset. "I asked everybody, including the janitors who worked in that building, to participate," said Ray, who is now retired. "The janitors were well aware of the financial position we were in."

In short order, through a series of experiences, the culture changed, and people wanted to do their part to help. They now understood how they could contribute, and they embraced the idea of One C-5.

A spirit of accountability took hold.

Here's one example: When the janitors were cleaning the floor of the warehouse where the aircraft were assembled, they didn't pay attention to things that got swept up and tossed in the trash. No big deal—something was on the floor, it was garbage. At least, that was the attitude before all this training, before they understood their part in the bigger picture.

One day, a janitor found several aircraft panel fasteners, the kind he and his colleagues regularly threw away without any consideration. In fact, Ray said, the janitor found large bags by the trash can; they were stuffed with these fasteners. The janitor didn't know what they were, but he had just gone through One C-5 workshops, where he had heard the McDonald's Story. So, he and some colleagues brought them to the floor manager.

"We know we're trying to cut costs," they said, showing the manager a handful of these fasteners. "We don't know what these are, but I want to bring them to your attention because they might be worth something, and they are all over the floor."

A single fastener, used in the assembly of sheet metal structures, costs a few dollars. But the team used thousands of them, and who knows how many were ending up in the garbage. The savings, especially over time, were considerable, although a tiny fraction of the overall cost of assembling the aircraft.

But more than the value was that this action represented the cultural shift Ray was after—the idea that everybody plays an important role in turning around this program and that the actions of a few janitors can help the entire organization. It all adds up to help cut costs and reduce schedule time, which is the goal when building a large aircraft for the military. Or, for that matter, when delivering the proper order at the drive-through. The customer expects it on time, as specified, at the agreed-upon price.

In one version of this story, the janitors could have been reprimanded for not having brought this up before. It's easy to imagine a floor manager scolding him, saying something like, "Are you kidding me?! You've been throwing those away? Those are valuable. No wonder we're so far behind and over budget."

Just like that, the floor manager would have created a belief that there's no point in chipping in. He could have focused on the fall instead of the step. But that's not what happened. The floor manager was grateful and enthusiastic, saying something like: "Oh my gosh, thank you for bringing that to our attention. That's exactly the kind of thing we need to know about."

Then the floor manager also gave the janitors recognition more broadly, sharing the story with his superiors and others.

Burick began sharing this story in workshops and staff meetings. The impact was swift: People on every team wanted to help out and began asking—and looking for—ways to reduce costs. It was a complete shift in behavior.

Within two years, the transformation was undeniable. The program overcame its $200 million deficit, met its delivery schedule, and restored customer confidence—all driven by a shift in shared Cultural Beliefs. Employees took ownership of their work, recognizing that their decisions directly impacted the success of the program.

Lockheed Martin's approach also had a ripple effect. The cultural model was adopted across other programs, and it became a cornerstone of the company's operational philosophy. While Ray's work to fix the C-5 program began a decade ago, the framework continues to this day across other programs within the aeronautics business of Lockheed Martin.

"The rest of the company took notice because of the success we had with the C-5 program," said Ray. The floor manager recognized the janitor and told the story to others. Ray shared it at town halls. The story spread. It wasn't just about the fasteners. It was about belief. And belief, as we know, drives behavior.

Here's the kicker: Storytelling is recognition. It's recognition that echoes beyond a performance review or a one-on-one conversation. When done well, storytelling turns moments of alignment into moments of transformation. It shines a spotlight on what good looks like and why it matters.

That's what makes storytelling one of the most powerful tools in culture management. And when it's done with intention and repetition, we call it Focused Storytelling.

Putting Focused Storytelling into Practice

Focused Storytelling is a culture management tool, and it is defined as: stories we purposefully and methodically tell about people and teams who demonstrate the Cultural Beliefs and impact R2 results.

These stories shape the organizational narrative. They spread beliefs. They drive alignment. And they work even if someone didn't experience the story firsthand. Hearing it is enough to shape how they think and act.

Focused Storytelling is a simple and powerful discipline. Here's how to do it:

1. **Start with the belief.** Use the language: *"Here's what [Cultural Belief] looks like to me."* This primes the listener. It tells them what to look for.
2. **Tell the story.** Keep it under forty-five seconds. Why? Because people tune out if you take too long. You want to hit hard and fast. One moment. One belief. One outcome.
3. **Connect to the result.** Link the behavior to your R2 Vision or Key Results. That's what makes it matter to the business.
4. **Close the loop.** End with: *"That's what [Cultural Belief] looks like to me."* You've now created a shared experience that reinforces belief.

And finally: Tell one story a week. That's what you can take accountability for. That's the practice. Done consistently, it aligns your team around the Results Equation.

After Lockheed Martin's C-5 transformation, employees summed it up perfectly: "It's the same location, but it's not the same place." That's what Focused Storytelling can do. It doesn't just spread information. It spreads belief. And belief is what gets you out of the command-and-control mindset—out of the Action Trap.

So, here's your challenge: Start looking for moments where someone lives your Cultural Beliefs and contributes to your R2 results. Use the language. Keep it short. Make the connection. Tell one story a week. Because stories change beliefs. Beliefs drive behavior. Behavior drives results.

That's what Focused Storytelling looks like to me.

For a quick reference on best practices to implement what you've learned in this chapter, visit surrendertolead.com/resources. There you will find our Focused Storytelling Best Practices Guide.

CHAPTER 13

FOCUSED FEEDBACK

Even Steph Curry still does shooting drills.

He's arguably the greatest shooter of all time. A four-time NBA champion. A two-time MVP. A household name. And yet, he's out there on the court, day after day, practicing the most basic skill in basketball.

Not because practice makes perfect but because he is seeking feedback. From his body. From the ball. From his coaches. From the technology.

It's not only about repetition—it's about refinement. Curry stays open to what the game is trying to teach him, even today. Even when you're on top, there's something new to learn.

Doug Merritt, CEO of cloud-networking company Aviatrix and former CEO of Splunk, approaches leadership the same way. He once told me (Jessica), "There is no failure. There is no success either. There's only learnings."

It's a bold mindset—especially coming from someone who's led multiple high-growth companies to extraordinary results. But that's exactly the point. Doug is a highly successful, results-driven leader *because* he doesn't obsess over outcomes. He focuses on effort, learning, and feedback, and the results follow.

That's exactly what psychologist Carol Dweck uncovered in her groundbreaking research on the growth mindset.[18] Dweck found that when people receive feedback focused on effort and learning rather than innate talent, they're more likely to persist, bounce back from failure, and improve over time. The growth mindset has reshaped how we think about success in both education and business. It reinforces the idea that feedback isn't just a performance review—it's a belief-shaping tool. It teaches people to see challenges not as setbacks, but as stepping stones.

That philosophy is at the heart of the SHIFT mindset: stop fighting reality, have faith, identify what you can control, free yourself from fear, and take the next right action.

When you live that way, you start to see what Doug sees. Success and failure are just labels. The real power is in the process. I often say, *I'm responsible for the effort. God is responsible for the outcome.* That's surrender. But it's not passive—it's focused. Strategic. And when you have the right tools, it becomes a results-driving superpower.

Doug leads from that place. As he puts it, "What makes a good dribble or pass in sports? Same thing at work—we need the coaching and feedback loops to master our craft."

He doesn't just say it—he builds entire cultures around it. Feedback isn't performance management to him—it's fuel. Insight. Collaboration. "Without feedback, this whole thing doesn't work," he says. And he means it.

When Doug joined Aviatrix, the sales strategy wasn't working. The team was trying to sell the full platform to every customer—an overwhelming approach that slowed growth. Instead of blaming or bulldozing forward, Doug got curious. He listened. He adapted. He shifted. And in doing so, he didn't just fix a sales motion—he transformed the culture.

The team shifted to a use-case-led selling approach. That change required a total rethinking of how people worked together, how they learned, and how they shared information.

For Doug, the key was focusing on learnings every single day. He restructured the sales org into cross-functional pods, combining account executives, systems engineers, business development reps, and partners. He implemented daily stand-ups and evening debriefs—not to report metrics, but to share what they learned that day. He added Monday/Wednesday/Friday all-hands learning reviews. Each team came forward with fresh insights: Which messaging landed? Which buyer persona missed the mark? What friction did we encounter?

At first, the rigor was met with resistance. People were uncomfortable admitting what they didn't know. Vulnerability doesn't come naturally in most corporate environments. But Doug held the line. Because this wasn't about perfection; it was about progress.

And it worked.

Doug had seen this pattern before. At Splunk, when he became CEO, cloud revenue was just 0.25% of the business. He knew the future was the cloud—but most of the company didn't. There was fear. Resistance. Skill gaps. Uncertainty. He didn't force it; he surrendered. He focused on creating experiences that would shift beliefs that the future was cloud. He listened. He asked questions. He turned the transition into a learning journey. Weekly stand-ups. Continuous feedback loops. Transparent conversations about what was working—and what wasn't. He stayed focused on what he could control, which was the experiences he was creating for the team.

Six years later, 60% of Splunk's bookings were cloud-based. The company had reinvented itself and was thriving. During his tenure as CEO, Doug led the transformation of Splunk from an on-premises perpetual-license software company with the equivalent of $220 million in annual recurring revenue (ARR) to a cloud-based SaaS company with ARR of $3.12 billion.[19]

Feedback doesn't have to be difficult. Doug says it best: "If learning is the goal, you'll for sure learn. And if you learn together, you'll get to a great outcome."

So, what does this mean for you?

It means feedback isn't something you wait to receive—it's something you actively seek.

Putting Focused Feedback into Practice

Doug's story is an example of how cultures that get results are built by design. And one of the most powerful design tools is Focused Feedback.

If storytelling spreads belief, feedback sharpens it. It brings clarity to intention. It tells you where you are and where you can grow. But only if you know how to give it—and how to receive it. And that is the key, receiving.

This chapter is not about how to give feedback; it's about how to ask for it. The SHIFT mindset is about letting go of your need to be right and to manage and control. Your best tool in driving alignment is asking for feedback, not giving it.

And there is an art to effective feedback requests. First, don't ask, "Do you have any feedback for me?" and then silently cross our fingers, hoping the answer is "Nope, you're good."

That's not accountability. That's insecurity dressed up as

humility. Free yourself from fear. To do that, you can assume that feedback exists and go after it. Ask, "What feedback do you have for me on how I handled X?"

It's a small shift in words and a big shift in mindset. It communicates that you are open. That you are hungry to learn. That you're not satisfied with the status quo.

And when you ask others for feedback, you give them permission to do the same. You create a loop—a rhythm—of learning and improvement that elevates everyone around you. And when you receive the feedback, avoid sending it through all of the filters we usually send feedback through: Is this accurate? Is this relevant? Is this pertinent? There's only one correct response to feedback: "Thanks for the feedback."

That's it. No rebuttal. No "Yeah, but . . . ." No "I already knew that." No explaining, no rationalizing, no dismissing. Just thanks.

Because when someone gives you feedback, they're offering a gift—whether it's wrapped in clarity or clumsiness. Your job isn't to decide whether they delivered it perfectly. Your job is to listen for the learning.

This is especially hard when the feedback hits a nerve. But that's when it's most important. That's when the growth happens.

And finally, feedback doesn't become power until you do something with it.

Take a moment to reflect. Ask yourself: What does this help me see? By acting on that feedback, you create an experience for the person who was willing to give it that will reinforce the belief that you are open to the feedback, and it will encourage more feedback. It will also open them up to asking for feedback themselves.

And if they do ask you for feedback, here are some best practices to keep in mind. Anchor yourself in love. Start with appreciative feedback. Acknowledge what the person is doing well. Be specific. Point to how their behavior supports your Cultural Beliefs or drives toward a Key Result.

Then offer constructive feedback—not by pointing out what went wrong, but by imagining what could go even better. Frame it around the future: "One thing that might help you demonstrate our Cultural Beliefs even more is . . . ."

You don't need to wait for a formal review cycle or leadership retreat. Focused Feedback is a daily habit. Start by asking three people for feedback this week. Remember to respond with, "Thanks for the feedback."

And then, model it.

Feedback is your unfair advantage—if you're brave enough to use it. Most people avoid it. Most cultures water it down. Most leaders pretend they want it but secretly hope to hear nothing. If you want to shift your mindset and your results, ask the question.

In my (Joe's) whole career, everyone always said feedback was important. And I'd nod and think, "No shit, Sherlock." Of course it is. But no one ever really showed me how to do it well—or how to receive it well, for that matter.

Before I joined Culture Partners, feedback was rare. And when it showed up, it was usually because something had gone off the rails. It felt like getting called out, not called forward.

What changed everything for me here was the framework. We don't just say feedback matters—we actually know how to do it. And the structure makes all the difference.

It starts with *appreciative feedback*. Real stuff. Not vague praise like "You're great," but specifics: "The way you laid out that client strategy helped us move forward with confidence." That builds trust. It helps the person know what to keep doing. And when someone knows you see the good in them, they're more open to hearing where they can grow.

Then—and only then—the constructive feedback. But it's not about what went wrong. It's not criticism. It's curiosity. It's, "Here's one thing that might help you be even more effective next time . . . ." That slight shift in language changes everything. It feels like support, not judgment. Appreciate first—because people need to know what's working. Then coach forward—because we all want to grow. That's it.

I used to brace for feedback like a two-by-four was coming at my head. Now? I want it. And most importantly, I ask for it often. When asking, I make sure the question is focused. For example, "What did you like about how I showed up at that meeting? How could I have made your experience better?" Because it's action-able. It's respectful. It's consistent. It's part of the culture, not some annual ritual. Asking for and providing feedback are two of the most powerful leadership tools in your bag!

I've gotten more real, helpful feedback at Culture Partners than in my entire career combined. And that's not just because people here are better at giving it—it's because the system supports it. We've built an environment that makes feedback safe, specific, and useful.

And I can tell you firsthand: Once you experience that, you never want to go back.

For a quick reference on best practices to implement what you've learned in this chapter, visit surrendertolead.com/resources. There you will find our Focused Feedback Best Practices Guide.

CHAPTER 14

REDUCING SILOS

The night before I (Jessica) was to give a keynote to a professional service company about how to shape culture to drive results, I was in the Bahamas, standing barefoot in the sand at a welcome party for the go-to-market team.

Music was playing, drinks were flowing. The demographic was young. The people were quick-witted. Sarcasm ran rampant. Jokes flowed. I immediately felt part of the team. There was a natural sense of trust and appreciation that told me this was a company with something special. They had a strong foundation: a shared understanding of their purpose, a clear strategy, and a leadership team committed to aligning the culture to support both. And they were ready to scale—fast.

The next morning, we kicked off the event. It was all about strategic execution—aligning culture to Key Results. Suzanne, the CEO, opened with clarity and force. She laid out three bold Key Results for the organization. Then she passed it over to me to talk about how to align their behaviors and beliefs with those Key Results—to turn their culture into a competitive advantage.

This team was used to moving fast, but they needed some alignment around moving together. I did the keynote, and then it was time to transition to the workshop portion of the experience. But before doing that, I opened it up for questions.

A hand shot up. A brave one. "Let's say, hypothetically," he began, "that two teams—say, sales and marketing—have a little trouble getting aligned." The room chuckled. You could feel the tension. He kept going. "Hypothetically, maybe sales feels like marketing doesn't respond fast enough with sales enablement materials. And maybe marketing keeps asking for insights from the field, but sales isn't really delivering."

Now the whole room was with him. Nervous grins. Nods. We weren't talking in hypotheticals anymore—we were naming the elephant in the room. He asked me what they should do. Instead of solving it for them, I asked a (perhaps controversial) question back, but one that I felt safe enough to ask given our time together the night before.

"What would it look like if you came from a place of love?"

Blank stares at first. I explained. "You just described both sides needing more. Sales needs faster turnaround. Marketing needs more intel. Everyone's focused on their own needs. That's scarcity thinking. That's fear. But what if you came from love instead?"

And then someone, remembering my keynote from earlier, said, "I guess we'd . . . ask for feedback?" Exactly.

Imagine a marketing team walking into a sales meeting—not with a request, not with a complaint—but with this question: "What feedback do you have for us on how we can better support you?"

No agenda. No defensiveness. Just curiosity. Just love the way Thomas Aquinas defined it, to will the good of another. I asked the group, "What do you think would happen next?" People started nodding. Someone said, "I'd be shocked . . . in a good way." Another said, "I'd want to reciprocate."

So, we didn't just talk about it. We did it. I split the room in half. Sales on one side. Marketing on the other. The assignment: ask for feedback—not as individuals, but as teams. One group listens, the other shares. Take notes. Break the feedback into themes. And most importantly—just say, "Thanks for the feedback." No rebuttals. No defense. Just gratitude.

The sales team went first, and what emerged was gold. Not just pain points, but solutions. Then they switched roles. Marketing asked, and sales delivered. It was a vulnerable, messy, powerful hour. This could have been useful enough, but we weren't done yet. The final step was alignment.

I introduced the framework that brings feedback into action and ties it directly to culture and results. Use the feedback to get in alignment. It looks like this:

"The belief I want you to hold about our team (or me) is . . ."
(For example: *We are standardizing to scale.*)

"Based on your feedback, the experience we're going to create for you is . . ."
(List the specific actions you're committing to—X, Y, Z.)

"If we do X, Y, and Z, will that be enough to shift your belief about us?"
(This is the feedback loop. The moment of alignment.)

In this case, the Cultural Belief was Standardize to Scale. The sales team, by asking for feedback, realized they were creating chaos by customizing solutions on the fly and overwhelming marketing with last-minute requests. If a client asked for a solution that didn't exist, they would pretend that it did and then send a note to marketing asking for a new asset.

From the sales perspective, it was a fast-growing, customer-obsessed, innovation-oriented approach. From the marketing perspective, it was whiplash. A constant stream of urgent, unvetted requests that bypassed strategy, ignored process, and left the team scrambling to keep up. It felt reactive, chaotic, and misaligned. The disconnect wasn't about intention—both teams wanted to win—it was about belief. Sales believed they were being scrappy and solution oriented. Marketing believed they were being steamrolled and under-resourced. And until those beliefs were surfaced, shared, and aligned, the silo would stay intact.

This very challenge was why the Cultural Belief of Standardize to Scale had been identified as a need in the first place. The company wasn't trying to stifle innovation or slow down momentum—it was trying to create sustainable growth. They needed to preserve the agility and customer obsession that had gotten them this far, while building the infrastructure and internal alignment that would carry them further. Standardization wasn't the enemy of speed—it was the foundation for scaling it.

A spokesperson for the sales team said, "The belief we want you to hold about us is that we are committed to standardizing to scale. The experiences we're going to create are giving marketing a weekly digest of customer insights; only requesting materials aligned to our official offerings; and attending one marketing team meeting a month to collaborate earlier in the cycle."

Then the salesperson asked, "If we do those three things, will that be enough to shift your belief?"

The answer doesn't have to be yes. Perhaps that's not enough. Marketing, in this case, also asked that all requests be filtered through a request portal rather than via email. The sales team agreed. And just like that, a silo became a bridge. Silos are not a structure problem—they're a mindset problem.

When teams operate in fear, scarcity, and self-protection, they build walls. But when they operate in love—yes, *love*—they build trust. Alignment isn't just about agreement. It's about mutual belief. And that doesn't happen with assumptions—it happens with intentional experiences. That's why feedback alone isn't enough. You need feedback, yes—but you also need a plan to act on it and a way to validate that it made a difference.

This is the alignment formula in action. Ask for feedback, say thank you, extract which experiences you need to create to shift their belief, and state the belief you wish to create and what experiences you will create to shift that belief. Finally, ask the magic question, "If I do those things, will that be enough to shift your belief?" If yes, great. Go do it. If not—ask what's missing.

This isn't just theory. We saw this same dynamic play out inside a high-growth, multi-billion-dollar energy company. The CEO came to us with a familiar challenge: silos. Sales was selling highly customized solutions, and they were doing it fast—but they feared the rest of the organization couldn't deliver on what they promised. Meanwhile, the rest of the org—engineering, operations, product—believed sales was out of control. Overpromising. Improvising. Creating chaos.

It wasn't a workflow problem. It was a trust problem. And underneath the mistrust was a lack of accountability. Each team was pointing fingers at the other. Sales thought delivery couldn't keep up. Delivery thought sales was setting them up to fail. No one was owning the shared problem.

We brought the teams together in a room—sales on one side, delivery on the other—and we ran the alignment process. They asked each other for feedback. They clarified the beliefs each team wanted the other to hold. And then they did the real work: creating experiences that could shift those beliefs.

What came out of that conversation wasn't a compromise—it was clarity. Together, they landed on a two-offering model that addressed customer needs while still being operationally executable. Sales could still win deals. Delivery could still follow through. And both sides had a hand in building the solution, which meant both sides were accountable for it.

They didn't just solve the silo problem. They proved what's possible when teams take ownership of the disconnect—when they choose trust over assumption, simplicity over chaos, and alignment over blame.

Do this regularly. Do it bravely. Do it from love, not fear. Start with one relationship—one team. Ask for feedback. Clarify the belief. Create the experience. Check for alignment. This is how silos fall. Not through hierarchy or process but through trust.

CHAPTER 15

SYSTEMS ALIGNMENT

When Vicente Reynal took the helm at Ingersoll Rand in 2015, he had an audacious goal: double the company's enterprise value in five years—from $3 billion to $6 billion. Ambitious, sure. But by 2021, something extraordinary had happened. The enterprise value wasn't just doubled; it was multiplied nine times over, ballooning from $3 billion to $27 billion. (As of March 2025, the company's enterprise value stood at about $37 billion.) How did they do it?

According to Reynal, their success was highly dependent on how effectively they linked their purpose, strategy, and performance-oriented culture to systems—business practices, for instance—moving the company forward.[20]

We've discussed experiences and their role in shaping culture and driving performance. However, it's important to clarify that there are actually three distinct types of experiences organizations can intentionally create:

Direct Experiences: These are immediate interactions—such as behaviors demonstrated by leaders or actions taken by team members—that employees directly observe and feel.

Narrative Experiences: These include third-party experiences conveyed through storytelling and recognition. Stories that circulate within the organization become powerful tools for shaping beliefs.

Systems Experiences: Often overlooked yet crucially important, these experiences emerge from the organizational systems themselves—such as business practices, technology, policies, procedures, incentive models, and structures.

We've explored direct and narrative experiences, but systems experiences deserve equal attention. Systems are critical because they consistently and systematically reinforce—or undermine—the purpose, strategy, and culture a company seeks to foster. Reynal's remarkable success at Ingersoll Rand underscores the immense value that comes when systems are deliberately aligned to reinforce all elements of the Results Equation.

Reynal wanted to take a bold approach. In May 2017, the company raised $826 million in its IPO. As part of the company's IPO, Reynal announced that all 6,000 employees would become owners of the company.

For Reynal, employee ownership became a core component to help drive their purpose, strategy, and culture. Then in 2020, when they acquired the industrial segment of Ingersoll Rand, the commitment to shared ownership deepened: $150 million of equity went to all 16,000 employees, equating to about 20% of their annual base salaries.

This wasn't a thank-you gift. Reynal wanted a deeper commitment to evaluating—and improving—all the systems and processes that make the company run. The workers, after all, are the ones who work where the problems are—and the bet was that as owners of the company (vs. straight employees), they'd feel a vested interest in making things run better.

This shift in thinking, from worker to owner, demanded another: an increase in transparency. Reynal wanted everyone to understand the financials, as they would understand their home budget. He invested in educating and training the workforce about what it means to "own" a part of the company, in financial concepts such as cashflow, and in sharing financial information all the way down to the front line. These experiences transitioned the employees' mindset from "This is a company I work for" to "This is my company," a powerful transformation that aligns personal goals with corporate objectives.

What happened next was profound. Employee engagement scores rocketed from below 20% to an astounding 90%. Safety incidents dropped by 71%, and employee attrition plummeted from 19% to just 3%. Vicente didn't simply issue equity—he aligned systems around a culture of ownership. "Value doesn't just come from senior leaders," he explained, "but from an entire population of experts moving together towards a common goal."

Pete Stavros, cohead of global private equity at KKR and the founder of the nonprofit Ownership Works, which advocates for employee-shared ownership, reinforced this point when I (Jessica) interviewed him: "Our experience is not only do these programs, when they're done effectively, change the feeling deep in the organization, but sometimes the biggest impact is at the top."[21]

The results speak for themselves: Ingersoll Rand estimates that aligning their systems around employee ownership added an additional $2.5 billion to their valuation. EBITDA margins improved by an impressive 700 basis points (7%), and its stock price tripled.

You might dream of innovation, but if your policy mandates six levels of approval for minor purchases, your people will naturally conclude "Innovation isn't valued here." Your system has unintentionally created a belief that stifles action.

You, as a leader, have to work to overcome this. This can begin with an audit of every system that impacts your employees' experience. Think beyond HR staples—recruitment, onboarding, training, and performance management—and extend it to approval processes, resource allocation, and financial transparency.

Then ask yourself (or better yet, your employees), "What beliefs are these systems unintentionally fostering?" If a cumbersome purchasing system suggests mistrust, simplify it. If opaque financial reporting breeds suspicion, clarify it. Vicente Reynal's leadership at Ingersoll Rand exemplifies the profound impact of integrating your purpose, strategy, and culture with thoughtful system design. Take this approach, and growth becomes not just a target but the outcome.

CHAPTER 16

PERSONAL RESULTS EQUATION

Every time I (Jessica) conduct an interview, whether it's for a job opening or a podcast guest, I always start with one pivotal question: "What's your why?" I ask because it is interesting and it adds depth to the dialogue, but I also ask to understand something deeper. Are we a fit?

You've probably heard a lot about the importance of "culture fit" in hiring and team dynamics. But culture fit is a myth. It suggests that hiring people who blend seamlessly into your company's existing environment fosters harmony and productivity. However, this concept is dangerously flawed. It narrows our vision, limits diversity, and stifles the very innovation it aims to cultivate by creating echo chambers of thought.

In the 1990s, investment bankers interviewing prospective candidates used to use the Airplane Test when they couldn't decide. The Airplane Test goes like this: If you had to be stuck sitting next to someone on a plane for five hours on the way to a client meeting, which candidate would you want to sit next to?

The Airplane Test is flawed because it directs you to make decisions based on who you'd rather get a beer with, rather than who is most aligned to your purpose, strategy, and culture. Most people end up choosing people just like them. Perhaps you went to the same college or are around the same age—it's a culture fit! You're just like me!

In my career, I've witnessed the limitations of the culture fit paradigm. It's a cozy but confining space where fitting in often overshadows standing out. The richness of diverse perspectives is sacrificed for the comfort of conformity.

So, what's the alternative? You need to champion *purpose* fit. This approach actively designs and cultivates an environment that not only embraces diversity but also fosters employee fulfillment.

Employee fulfillment is employee engagement 2.0. Employee engagement is a trap. Employee engagement is an antiquated concept that's losing relevance in the modern workplace. Originating in the 1990s, the term "employee engagement" was popularized by management consultants who pitched it as a golden metric for CEOs eager to boost productivity through enhanced focus and task adherence. The word *engagement* means to focus on the task at hand. It was an attractive proposal: Focus on engagement and watch your workforce's productivity skyrocket. Yet, this approach is fundamentally flawed—it's trapped in a cycle of action without deeper alignment or meaning.

In the 1980s, we spoke about job satisfaction—a simpler, albeit less dynamic measure of how content people felt with their jobs. But culture isn't about feelings either. Culture is about beliefs that drive actions to deliver results. As the corporate world evolved, so did the terminology and strategies surrounding workforce management. Job satisfaction gave way to employee engagement, a term that implied a deeper connection to one's work but still focused primarily on the physical act of working, not on the emotional or intellectual commitment to the work.

That's why you must move beyond engagement to employee fulfillment. Fulfillment digs deeper, asking not just "Are you engaged?" but "Are you fulfilled?" It's about understanding how achieving personal purpose aligns with achieving organizational purpose. This alignment is crucial because when employees see their work contributing to a larger goal that resonates with their values, they are naturally more motivated, productive, and satisfied.

To find this alignment, you need to understand that just as your company has a Results Equation, each employee has the opportunity to create their own Personal Results Equation.

Consider the Personal Results Equation each of us carries within. Everyone has their own purpose. You also have long-term goals (R2 Vision). You have personal Key Results to measure your professional success throughout the year and Personal Drivers that focus your priorities as well as Core Beliefs that drive your own actions. When a company's environment and culture nurture these personal elements, aligning them with the organization's overarching goals, it sets the stage for profound and sustainable impact.

But here's the part most leaders miss: You can't lead your company, department, or team through the Results Equation if you haven't walked that path yourself. To authentically create experiences that drive purpose, strategy, and culture for your organization, you need to be clear on what those mean in your own life. Leadership isn't performance—it's alignment. And alignment starts with you.

Ask yourself:

Purpose	What is my purpose?
R2/Vision	Where do I want to be in five years?
Key Results	What results am I pursuing this year?
Personal Drivers	What drivers will get me there?
Core Beliefs	What beliefs must I live by to stay aligned and accountable to that vision?

This is your Personal Results Equation. It's not just a worksheet—it's a mirror. And until you can look into it and see yourself clearly, you won't be able to lead others to do the same. So, before you bring this framework to your team, bring it to your own life.

Define your Personal Results Equation. Write it down. Revisit it weekly. Let it become your compass.

Your Personal Results Equation is:

Purpose + Drivers + Beliefs = Results

(To download a Personal Results Equation Builder, visit surrendertolead.com/resources or scan the QR code at the beginning of the book.)

Here's what mine (Jessica's) looks like:

Purpose	My purpose is to serve God and others.		
R2/Vision	My R2 Vision is to have ten years sober on December 11, 2030.		
Key Results	Do girl chat with Ellie every night we are together.	Impact five million lives with the power of surrender.	Finish another year sober.
Personal Drivers	Spiritual	Physical	Service
Core Beliefs	Serve: I aim to be useful.	Love: I choose love over fear.	Surrender: I am a vehicle for God's will, not my will.

Once you've done the work, you're ready to lead others through it. Invite your team to create their own Personal Results Equation. But don't just tell them to do it—model it. Be vulnerable. Be human. That's how alignment begins. Because the truth is, every individual at your company isn't just filling a role. They are fulfilling a personal destiny. And when that destiny aligns with your organization's mission, something incredible happens: People stop working for the company and start working as the company.

I (Jessica) have lived this alignment in the most personal way.

When my dad died, he died alone of an aortic dissection (a tear in a large blood vessel branching off of the heart) in an elevator. That moment shattered me. The grief was overwhelming, but it also cracked me open. In that pain, I found clarity: I felt that healing would take place if I could make sure fewer people left this world alone.

That realization led me to volunteer for UC Davis's No One Dies Alone program, where volunteers sit with patients who are at end of life but have no friends and family. Volunteers take turns sitting in four-hour shifts so each patient has someone present with them until the very end. That work felt like the most sacred thing I'd ever done.

After five years of volunteering at UC Davis, I learned about a new initiative in my neighborhood that was breaking ground. Joshua's House is the first hospice for unhoused people on the entire West Coast. In order to qualify for hospice, people need a prognosis of six months or less to live and a place for care. Unhoused individuals don't have a place for care, and so they don't qualify and are sent out on the streets to die unmedicated and alone. This organization was determined to change that.

When I heard they were opening in July 2025, I raised my hand to volunteer both as a death doula and a volunteer chaplain. Many of the people they serve struggle with addiction, mental illness, and cycles of trauma—experiences I deeply understand and feel connected to. Some of my greatest mentors and friends have lived those same stories and, in recovery, found strength.

What made Joshua's House unique was that they were building something new—no legacy systems, no inherited culture. Together, we created their first Results Equation. It became more than a tool for operations; it guided how they recruited volunteers and employees, inspired fundraising, and told their story to the community.

Here is their Results Equation:

Purpose	To give humanity a home.		
R2/Vision	To inspire five other similar homes in the next five years.		
Key Results	Achieve an eight-patient average daily census by end of year.	Complete a Launch Resource Toolkit by end of year.	Break even financially by end of year.
Strategic Drivers	We honor our residents.	We measure our impact.	We foster positive employee experiences.
Cultural Beliefs	I celebrate diversity.	I take accountability.	I am an adaptive learner.

When I looked at their equation and compared it to mine, I felt a profound sense of alignment. Their purpose (to give humanity a home) fit perfectly with mine—to serve God and others. Their cultural beliefs mirrored my own commitments to service, love over fear, and surrender to something bigger than myself.

This alignment lit me up. It made me care deeply—not just about what Joshua's House was building but about who I was becoming as I served there. That's the magic: when your personal Results Equation aligns with your organization's, fulfillment follows.

This isn't about culture fit. This is about purpose fit. Fulfillment. Alignment. It starts with you. By breaking free from outdated paradigms and embracing a future where fulfillment and alignment lead the way, we can transform not just workplaces but lives. This is the crux of why we must surrender to the truth—because in truth, there is freedom. Freedom to grow, to contribute meaningfully, and to build a culture that resonates deeply with every individual's core being.

Remember, every individual at your company is not just filling a role; they are here to fulfill a personal destiny that can—and should—align with your organization's mission. If they don't, then perhaps it's not a good fit. Engage in these conversations, encourage your teams to fill out their Personal Results Equations, and watch as your company transforms into a dynamic ecosystem where everyone is empowered to contribute their best.

And remember that it always starts with you. What's your why?

CHAPTER 17

CASCADING CHANGE

The most common question we get after keynotes is, "This sounds great, but what do I do if my leader isn't on board?"

You are in control of yourself, not others. And yet, this is where so many people get stuck. Just as it is ineffective for leaders to continually blame employees for not working differently, it's also damaging for employees to keep blaming their CEO. You may have those thoughts as you read through this book: *If only my boss would take this on, things would be different.*

It is easy to get caught up in the frustration of waiting for someone else to take the lead. But that frustration is wasted energy. You cannot force others into action. Managing up is no more effective than managing down when it comes to inspiring real change.

Take Kobe Bryant, for example.

In 2008, the US men's Olympic basketball team was filled with stars. But it was Kobe who changed the culture. While others were sleeping, he was in the gym at 4:00 a.m.—running, lifting, shooting. Not once. Every day.

At first, teammates thought it was overkill, choosing to go

out and party late into the night—so late that when they came home, they passed him in the hall on his way back from an early morning workout. Over time, they started joining him. One by one, the late nights stopped. Early mornings started. No lectures. No demands. Just discipline that inspired the rest to rise to his level.

That team didn't just win gold—they redefined what it meant to lead: through example, not authority.

Shift to surrender. Stop fighting reality—your boss is not on board. Have faith but not in an abstract sense. Have faith in the process itself. Identify what is yours. Right now, in this moment, you have a team to lead. Free yourself from fear. Put your team's needs first, not your own. Wishing your boss would lead with love is well intentioned, but it's still you trying to control what is uncontrollable. And finally, take the next right action. You have the power to create meaningful change, even if you're not at the top of the org chart.

As a leader, you have the power to shape the experiences of others. And when you lead your team with clarity, alignment, and accountability—anchored in your purpose, strategy, and culture—you're not just influencing your direct reports.

You're creating an experience *for the very executives you wish would change.*

You don't have to wait for a top-down mandate that may never come. You can model the shift now. When your team becomes a living example of what's possible through focus, ownership, and results, you start to influence upward. You create culture by design, not by permission.

One of the best examples of a cascading change came from Hormel Foods, a $16 billion global branded food company with around 20,000 employees. They had built their success on a portfolio of brands like Skippy®, SPAM®, Applegate®, and Planters®. But like any large organization that grows through acquisition, the culture experienced in one division sometimes looked different than another. Large organizations are made of many microcultures; this is normal.

But one manager had a massive impact on the company at large. This particular manager didn't just read *The Oz Principle*, the first book written by the founders of our firm—he lived it. Inspired by the power of personal accountability, he began applying the concepts to his own leadership first. Then he brought those same ideas to his division, embedding the principles of accountability into the way his team operated.

This wasn't just theory. It showed up in performance. The division thrived, and people noticed.

At the time, Jim Snee wasn't yet CEO, but he saw what was happening. He was impressed—not just by the results but by how the culture itself had shifted. Employees weren't just doing their jobs; they understood how their work connected to Key Results. They had a language for accountability that wasn't punitive but empowering. And it was contagious.

As Jim rose through the ranks and eventually became CEO in 2016, he remembered what he had seen. He understood that what had started as a small spark could become a guiding light for the entire company. So he made the decision to unify the organization under one set of Cultural Beliefs. This clarity brought the company together—it was aligned, speaking the same common language, and grounded in a culture of accountability and performance. What began with one leader and one division became a company-wide movement.

Importantly, at Hormel, there was no heavy-handed mandate. Jim encouraged the change, but it spread because it worked.

This story reflects an essential truth that Greg Satell describes in his book *Cascades: How to Create a Movement That Drives Transformational Change.* He explains that this kind of transformation doesn't unfold in a straight line from the top, which is how most organizations think of change. We are at point A, but we need to go to point B. Let's create a plan to get there. Then we will roll it out through a series of communications and training plans.

In fact, when people are forced to adopt an initiative in this manner, they usually resist. But when small, passionate groups take accountability and create undeniable success, others naturally want to be part of that success. And eventually they become its champions.

This is exactly what happened at Hormel Foods. The Results Equation wasn't forced onto people; it pulled them in.

So, what does this mean for you?

If you're sitting in a company where the leadership team isn't fully on board, you have two choices. You can feel helpless, or you can shift your thinking.

Remember—people don't change behaviors because they're told to. They change because they experience something that shifts how they see the world—or, in this example, how they see and experience their team at work. Let success do the talking. When others see how your team is thriving, they'll take notice. And that's when the pull effect begins.

You don't need permission to create alignment within your own team. Start small. Pick your department, your team, your division—whatever you have influence over. Define your Results

Equation. Get clarity on the Key Results that matter and align your culture around them. Create experiences that shape beliefs.

You may not be able to change an entire company in a few weeks, or even months, but you can create undeniable momentum in your own sphere of influence.

That's how movements start. That's how cultural transformation takes hold. And that's how organizations don't just implement change but become it.

PART THREE

ACCOUNTABILITY

CHAPTER 18

ABOVE THE LINE

In October 2017, I (Joe) was fired.

I had just led the company over a period of almost ten years through major growth. We had delivered record results, built a strong team, and positioned ourselves for the next phase of expansion. But the moment came—a crossroads. I believed we needed to go in one direction. My private equity partners, who had acquired the company two years earlier, wanted to go in another.

In five minutes, it was over. I understood. This is how the game is played. We shook hands and cordially went our separate ways.

I walked through the front door of my house that afternoon still processing what had just transpired. Even though I had an idea it was coming, I took it hard. As I entered, my wife, Katie, greeted me with a sympathetic look. I had called her on my way home, and she knew what happened.

As I walked through the door, she handed me a certified letter that had just arrived that day. I opened it and laughed at the irony. It was an invitation from HKW—the private-equity group that had sold the company to the new PE firm in 2015—inviting me to their annual investor meeting to be inducted into their Hall of Fame for "demonstrating exceptional leadership, talent, integrity, and remarkable shareholder return."

You can't make this stuff up. I had just been fired . . . and celebrated all in the same breath. The irony of it all hit me like a gut punch laced with comedy. One group was honoring my exemplary leadership. The other had just voted me off the island. What do you even *do* with that? The answer: You learn, and you focus on what you can control.

This moment became one of the clearest examples in my life of the principle we teach at Culture Partners—the idea of Above the Line and Below the Line thinking.

You know how the saying goes: You don't always get to choose what happens to you. But you *do* get to choose how you interpret it and how you react and respond. That choice is what accountability is all about. Accountability is such a powerful and freeing concept. However, when people say the word "accountability," what they often mean is: *Who's to blame? Who was responsible?*

Accountability isn't about blame, it's not a weapon for someone else to own, and it's not a management tool to force people to improve performance. It's a personal choice, a mindset, and a commitment to live Above the Line—to focus on what you can control and take ownership for driving the results that matter. When you embrace this 100% (not 50% or 90% but 100%), it becomes a powerful source of liberation.

You must be 100% accountable before you can ask others to be accountable.

At Culture Partners, when we begin working with a new leader, we typically ask two questions:

1. How are you doing on your results?
2. How is your energy?

And more often than not, we hear the same thing: "I'm exhausted. My team just won't take accountability." And I get it. You want people to *own it.* You want them to drive the ball forward without you always having to be the one pushing. But let's pause for a second and ask the harder question: Why do you want them to take accountability?

Because if we're being honest, command-and-control leadership is exhausting; constantly checking on people and what they're doing is a heavy lift. So, we long for a team that just gets it—people who take initiative and do the right things without being told.

But here's the thing: People don't take accountability because they're told to. They take accountability when they believe it's theirs to take.

And belief is born out of experience. This is where Above the Line thinking comes in.

Above the Line vs. Below the Line

The founders of Culture Partners, Tom Smith and Roger Connors, introduced a simple but powerful framework years ago: The Line. It was first revealed in their bestselling 1994 book *The Oz Principle: Getting Results Through Individual and Organizational Accountability.*

Decades later, *The Oz Principle* still sells thousands of copies every month. It has become a timeless classic—one of the most enduring books about accountability in business history.

So, what exactly is The Line?

The Line represents a clear distinction between two radically different mindsets—Above the Line thinking (ownership, accountability, action) and Below the Line thinking (blame, excuses, denial).

Below the Line is where blame lives. Excuses. Denial. Finger-pointing. It's the land of "it's not my fault" and "someone else dropped the ball."

Sound familiar?

This is the language of disempowerment—of people who have surrendered not to leadership but to their own helplessness. This is where fear and ego live.

Above the Line, on the other hand, is where ownership lives. It's where people take initiative, lean into challenges, and ask, *What else can I do to move this forward?* It's not about perfection. It's about ownership. It's the difference between reacting and responding. Between deflecting and doing. This is leading with love and abundance.

This framework has endured for a reason—it's immediately recognizable. Everyone knows what it feels like to be Below the Line (we've all been there), and everyone wants to lead—and be part of—a team that consistently operates above it. But here's the hard truth: You can't get people Above the Line by force. You get them there by modeling it—and by creating the conditions where ownership becomes the natural response.

You can't just *tell* people to think a certain way. At least not if you want it to have meaning. You have to create the *conditions* for them to choose it. Getting people Above the Line doesn't start with them—it starts with *you*. You can only control the experiences you create. Accountability isn't something you demand from others. It's something you demonstrate yourself, especially when things go sideways.

For me, that lesson wasn't just learned in a boardroom—it was also earned on the Ironman course.

Given my long history as an Ironman athlete, it might surprise you to hear that I don't like to swim, bike, or run.

But I *love* the process, what each training session and ultimately each race teaches me. Every Ironman race is a microcosm of life compressed into a ten-to-twelve-hour period. With so many ups, downs, challenges, and breakthroughs, it trains the mind and body how to prepare for and work through adversity. And nothing has taught me more about Above the Line thinking—about choosing 100% ownership in the face of adversity—than racing.

Why? Because Ironman isn't about the outcome; it's about the process. It's about pushing yourself to the edge and discovering what you're made of when everything in you wants to stop. It's a masterclass in personal accountability.

Waking up at 4:30 a.m. to swim before work. Logging one-hundred-mile bike rides when everyone else is at brunch. Running when your legs feel like concrete. No one's making me do it, and no one is seeing me do it. There's no one to blame when I skip a workout and no one to applaud me when I complete one. It's just me, 100% accountable to the process, not the outcome. And every race is a reflection of life. There are moments when you feel unstoppable— and moments when you hit the wall. But you have trained and prepared for this, so you keep going in the face of adversity.

I remember one of the lowest points in my career—not in a race but in life. This was way before I started racing Ironman, when my company imploded during the dotcom bust of 2000. The pressure was greater than I had ever felt. I had very young twin daughters and no real road map for what was next.

At that moment I thought I had failed. But just as in a race, when you believe you might not be able to take one more step, feeling like you are at the doorstep of failure, there comes a breakthrough. That was the catapult to one of the most successful stretches in my career. That moment, upon reflection, birthed a new belief: Resilience is a muscle. It can be trained, and—most importantly—you can train on your terms, so that when adversity strikes, you are ready. And just like any muscle, accountability is something you work at and improve.

At first glance, the idea of accountability may appear to be at odds with the concept of surrender. If surrender means letting go, releasing control, and accepting what is, then how can it possibly coexist with a principle that demands ownership, responsibility, and forward motion?

This perceived contradiction is understandable—and it's one of the most common misconceptions we encounter when teaching this work. On the surface, surrender and accountability seem like two opposing forces: one rooted in acceptance, the other in action. One invites release; the other appears to require resolve. One says, "Let go." The other says, "Step up."

But look deeper, and a powerful truth emerges:

Surrender is not the opposite of accountability. It is the very foundation that makes accountability possible. Because you cannot truly become accountable until you surrender to the reality of what you can control and what you can't.

If you're still fighting circumstances you can't change—blaming the market, your boss, your colleagues, the system, the economy—you're not accountable. You're Below the Line. You've given your power away. You're stuck in a loop of denial, excuses, and justification.

Surrender clears the fog. It's the moment you say, "This is

happening. I don't control it. But I do control how I respond. I surrender to reality and will stop fighting what is."

That's where real accountability begins. It's not about controlling everything. It's about owning what's yours—and letting go of the rest.

That's why the SHIFT model is so powerful:

- **Stop fighting reality**—Acknowledge what's true, even if it's uncomfortable.
- **Have faith**—Trust that you can move forward without knowing the full path.
- **Identify what's yours**—Take ownership of your mindset, your actions, and your next step.
- **Free yourself from fear**—Let go of ego, judgment, and the need for certainty. Step into love.
- **Take the next right action**—Do what's within your power, with integrity and purpose.

That's not weakness. That's leadership. What looks like surrender from the outside is 100% ownership from the inside. It's not about letting go of *responsibility*. It's about letting go of the illusion that you can control people, places, or things.

In the end, leadership is about accepting what you cannot control while having the courage to change what you can. Yes, we realize it sounds like the Serenity Prayer, which packs important lessons in a single sentence. Forget about its connection to twelve-step programs; its message is universal. The first printed version, in fact, appeared in the 1944 Book of Prayers and Services for the Armed Forces, published by the US government during World War II.[22] It read:

God, grant me the serenity to accept the things I cannot change, the courage to change the things I can, and the wisdom to know the difference.

The leaders who succeed—those who inspire, drive results, and create lasting impact—are the ones who constantly evolve, challenge their own thinking, and operate from a place of purpose and faith rather than fear and a desire to achieve more and more power.

Surrender strips away the noise so accountability can take root. It's not passivity. It's clarity.

One of the most revealing insights from our research came when we surveyed over 30,000 leaders across industries and asked a simple question: Do you consider yourself accountable? An overwhelming 85% said yes.

But when asked if their *teams* are accountable? That number drops to 13%.

Everyone thinks they're the exception. That *they* are the one carrying the load while everyone else is slacking off. That *they* get it and everyone else is Below the Line. But the real problem isn't just lack of accountability. It's a lack of clarity and alignment. We're stuck in a blame loop. That's why your job as a leader isn't to demand more accountability—it's to model it. Speak the language. Create the environment. Show people what Above the Line looks like.

When I got fired in 2017, I had a choice. I could have gone Below the Line—blamed my PE partners, stewed in resentment, and told myself I'd been wronged. Or I could go Above the Line—accept what was, focus on what I could control, and move forward with purpose.

Three years later, that choice paid off. HKW—the same firm that inducted me into their Hall of Fame—called me back. They had acquired Culture Partners (at that time it was called Partners in Leadership) and asked if I would come on board to lead the company. It was a company with a purpose that aligned with my purpose and gave me an opportunity to impact lives all over the world. Everything had come full circle.

Above the Line is about love and abundance. It doesn't guarantee the future. It doesn't promise fairness. But it always prepares you for the opportunity when it comes. And it always leads you toward the next right action.

CHAPTER 19

STEPS TO ACCOUNTABILITY

If you've made it this far, you know this truth: Control is a lie, and culture—not commands—drives results. Surrendering the illusion of control doesn't mean letting go of responsibility. It means doing the deeper work: shaping the experiences that form beliefs, which drive action and, ultimately, create results.

That's why accountability matters. Not as a tool for blame but as a practice of ownership, clarity, and empowerment. A culture of accountability doesn't emerge from yelling louder, humiliating people, or holding more meetings. It emerges when people begin to see clearly, own their part, solve what's in front of them, and do what needs to be done.

We call this process *See It, Own It, Solve It, Do It*. SOSD, for short. It is the antidote to the blame game. And it's the cornerstone of sustainable cultural transformation.

Let us show you what it looks like in real life.

See It

When we began working with CNH Industrial, a multinational manufacturer of agricultural and construction equipment, the lack of trust among the top leaders quickly became apparent. At the time, they had just appointed a new CEO—one of four in six years—and half of the senior leadership team was also new. There was a deep "old versus new" divide in the organization.

Tension simmered across every level—between regional offices, across continents, and especially between US operations and global headquarters in London. The leadership team was fragmented, skeptical, and misaligned. People weren't collaborating—they were pointing fingers. This is what it looks like when a company is stuck Below the Line.

We began with an anonymous trust assessment, asking senior executives to rate each other's reliability and integrity. The results were stark: lots of Ds and Fs. Before we could do anything else, we had to rebuild trust from the ground up. That starts with seeing the truth, no matter how uncomfortable it is.

We call this the first step to accountability: See It.

Once you see reality for what it is, you can stop fighting it and instead take accountability for building an environment of clarity, alignment, and accountability—all in service to others across the organization to help them reach their potential.

This means moving from a place of externalizing blame to internalizing the need for change. It means you move from telling people what to do to engaging the hearts and minds of those on the mission with you.

The concept of accountability is often associated with blame and, as a result, punishment. But that's not how we think of it. Accountability is simply a powerful motivator for achieving the results you want. It is not something someone else does to you; it's something you do for yourself, your team, and your organization to help you grow and get better results. That attitude is a call for people to step up and own their behavior. One approach holds you and your organization back. The other inspires and unleashes the potential in people, the heights of which they never knew possible.

Own It

With 40,000 employees across the globe, CNH Industrial wasn't aligned under a unified vision, and it had become fragmented and messy as a result of spinoffs and mergers. (CNH is the product of a merger with Fiat.)

Scott Wine, then the CEO, came to us with a sense of urgency because, in our language, people spent most of their time Below the Line. "It took me about two weeks to realize that the bureaucracy was so thick we had to find a way to cut through it," he explained on an episode of our podcast, *Culture Leaders: The Masters Behind Movements*.[23]

That realization fueled Wine's drive to change the culture and remove barriers to decision-making. "We've got a culture of people pointing fingers, blaming the new CEO, blaming the old CEO, blaming this person or that person, blaming the industry," he said.

We began with a half-day workshop at CNH's Chicago office. The session, centered around the Results Pyramid framework, helped executives see the gap between their current behaviors and the outcomes they wanted. The immediate focus was on identifying and aligning around Key Results. Narrowing down priorities from an overwhelming list of thirty priorities to just the Key Results was a significant early victory.

During the session, the underlying beliefs holding the orga-nization back became clear: resistance to change, a preference for siloed thinking, and a tendency to blame external factors such as market conditions or previous leadership. By helping leaders articulate these challenges, the team began to replace these limiting beliefs with empowering ones. These were their C1 to C2 shifts.

But the success of any cultural transformation hinges on more than a rollout plan. Systems can shift. Language can evolve. Training can happen. But none of it matters if the people at the top aren't modeling the change themselves.

That's where Scott Wine came in. A graduate of the United States Naval Academy with deep roots in the aerospace industry, Wine brought a leadership style grounded in discipline, integrity, and service. He believes—fiercely—that leaders must set the tone, not just through words, but through consistent action. "Once you breach that integrity," he explained, "it gives permission to other people in the organization to do the same."

When asked about his why—what motivates him as a leader—Wine pointed to his upbringing. "My why is pretty darn simple," he said. "I was very blessed to grow up in the small town of Dayton, Virginia, and faith and family have always been important to me.

"When I was at the Naval Academy, I decided that I needed to or wanted to go to chapel every Sunday. And the why—my why—is best captured in a sentence from the Midshipman's Prayer:

> Keep me true to my best self, guarding me against dishonesty in purpose and in deed and helping me so to live that I can stand unashamed and unafraid before my shipmates, my loved ones, and thee.

"That really just encapsulates what drives me. I'm ridiculously competitive, but I try to keep that competitiveness toward the right thing, just knowing that those values are so important." He also sticks to a rigorous personal routine, such as daily workouts, to maintain the focus and energy needed to drive cultural transformation.

Wine didn't just lead the change. He owned it.

Solve It

But ownership without action is just a good intention.

Once leaders take responsibility, they must identify the real barriers to progress and start solving them—not just reacting to symptoms but addressing the root causes that stand in the way of results.

Wine observed that CNH was too focused on internal problems. He borrowed a method from Kevin Sharer, the former CEO of Amgen, who cowrote *The CEO Test: Master the Challenges That Make or Break All Leaders*, to get to the heart of the problems. The book uses a series of questions designed to break down the issues facing highly complex organizations.

Wine asked hundreds of employees five key questions to diagnose the organization's issues. They were:

1. What three things do you want me to change?
2. What three things do you want me to protect?
3. What are you worried I might do?
4. What do you want me to do?
5. What else do you want to talk about?

To his surprise—shock, really—not a single response mentioned customers. That revealed a monumental problem. This stark realization drove CNH's renewed focus on customers, which became a cornerstone of CNH's cultural transformation.

Additionally, Wine emphasized the importance of agility in decision-making. "I'd rather be 60% right and move fast than 100% right and move too slow," he said. This mindset helped CNH break through bureaucratic inertia, instilling a culture where employees felt empowered to make decisions and take ownership.

Do It

With clarity around the problem and alignment around new beliefs, it was time to act. That's what the final step—Do It—is all about. It's where accountability becomes habit. Where talk becomes behavior. Where the culture comes to life.

What followed was an ambitious rollout of the Results Equation across CNH's global operations. The program trained over 600 "Culture Champions," employees who acted as stewards of the company's new Cultural Beliefs. Within nine months, every one of CNH's employees had participated in the training—a monumental effort that demonstrated the company's commitment to embedding accountability at every level.

We had people frame desired results through a series of clear, action-oriented questions. Eventually, employees embraced the removal of bureaucratic barriers, eager to move faster and focus more on customer needs. This alignment energized the workforce, creating a ripple effect that improved both internal dynamics and external perceptions. New Cultural Beliefs were created, starting—naturally—with putting the customer first, but also encouraging the company to act as "one team" and to "be the best."

CNH saw immediate benefits. Regions like South America, which had already built a strong culture around customer focus, became examples for others to emulate. Operational metrics like quality and customer satisfaction improved, and the company was better positioned to navigate market challenges.

"I'm really proud of what we did," said Wine. "We had over 40,000 employees that bought into our Cultural Beliefs and really recognized the importance they had, every single one of them, in serving our customers. You could feel the difference in how we reacted."

Wine took to LinkedIn to summarize his pride:

Scott Wine ☑ · 2nd   **+ Follow** ···
CEO | Investor | Board Member | Leader
2yr · 🌐

I am incredibly proud of our CNH team for the impressive results they delivered in 2022: Revenue up 21% to $23.6B, over $2B of Net Income and Cash Flow of $1.6B. But I am most appreciative of how they did it – through relentlessly delivering for our customers, enhancing our culture and being accountable for results, we won the right way, every day. Our future is bright as our 38k employees work to realize the aspirations on the graphic below, for the benefit of our customers and dealers around the world!
#cnhindustrial #customersfirst #accountability #culture

Making It Yours

The transformation at CNH shows what's possible when leadership embraces accountability from the top. But SOSD isn't just for executives. Culture shifts when everyday behaviors shift. Because your behavior is someone else's experience that shapes a belief.

No matter your role, you're contributing to your organization's culture every day. The way you respond to a missed deadline, a poor result, a tough conversation, or an unclear expectation—that's culture. It's not what's written on the wall. It's what happens in the hall. And it starts with the small, seemingly ordinary choices we make in our work and in our relationships.

It starts with a moment. A moment where something goes sideways. A project fails, or a teammate drops the ball, or someone says something that doesn't sit right. In that moment, the natural human instinct is to protect ourselves—to explain, deflect, or point the finger. But this is where the shift happens. This is where culture begins to change.

Instead of reacting, we pause. And we *see it*.

We tell the truth about what's actually happening, without the mental gymnastics or justifications. We get curious, not defensive. We ask ourselves, "What's the reality here? What's really going on?" And we do it with compassion—for ourselves and others. This is the first move in SOSD. And it's the first move in SHIFT. It's a surrender to reality. An unflinching look at the truth, not to assign blame, but to open the door to change.

Once we see it, the next step is to *own it*. That means taking responsibility—not for everything, but for what's ours. It's easy to fall into the trap of victimhood. To believe we're powerless, or that the problem is someone else's to fix. But accountability is an act of faith. Faith that our choices matter. Faith that in this moment we can learn something. Faith that everything happens for a reason. And so, we ask, "What part of this is mine?" We identify what's ours.

From that place of ownership, we can begin to *solve it*. Not from fear but from love. Fear says, "Don't speak up; you might make it worse." Fear says, "You'll sound foolish. It's not your job." But love says, "This matters. Let's try." Love invites collaboration, creativity, and optimism. Solving it doesn't mean fixing everything. It means asking, "What's the outcome I want? And what's one thing I can do to move us in that direction?" You don't need to be the boss to bring a solution to the table. You just need the courage to care enough to try.

And then—most importantly—you *do it*. You take the next right action. You don't wait for someone else to go first. You follow through on what you said you'd do. You check in. You keep your word. This is where your integrity lives—not in what you say but in what you choose to do next. It doesn't need to be a grand gesture. It can be as simple as sending the email you've been avoiding. Giving feedback with kindness. Asking the hard question. Acting in alignment with what you've seen, owned, and worked to solve.

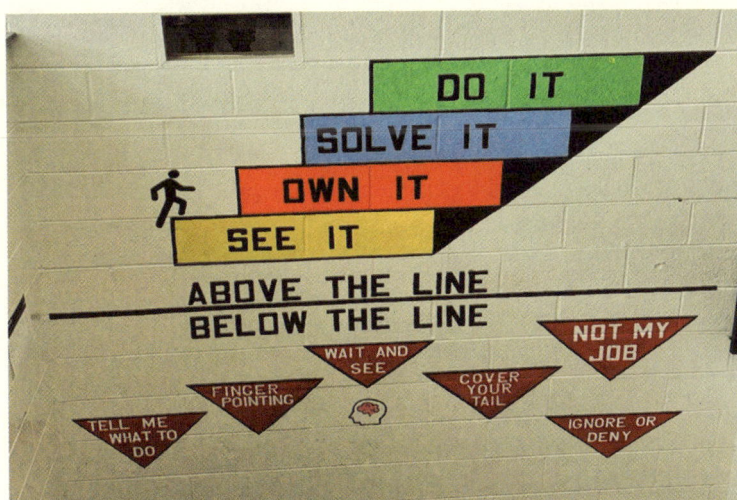

This is what SOSD looks like in real life. It's not a framework you apply once a quarter in a strategy session. It's a way of moving through the world. And when you practice it—not perfectly but consistently—you change not only your culture but your own sense of self. Because accountability, at its core, is an act of love. Love for the mission. Love for the people you serve. And love for your own growth. It's not always comfortable. But it is always worth it.

So don't wait for someone else to model it. Start with yourself. One moment. One shift. One right action at a time.

That's how culture changes. That's how people change. And that's how you become a leader—no title required.

For a quick reference on best practices to implement what you've learned in this chapter, visit surrendertolead.com/resources. There you'll find our Accountability Best Practices Grading Sheet.

CHAPTER 20

HELPING OTHERS BECOME ACCOUNTABLE

Every morning, I (Jessica) drive my eight-year-old daughter to school. She sits in the backseat, immersed in her tablet—a daily routine that's peaceful until we hit the speed bump.

The speed bump is about a third of the way to school, and it jostles the car. Every morning her finger slips, and her game character stumbles or falls. With remarkable predictability, she says, "You made me lose my game!" Her frustration is palpable, her blame instinctive. This, in its essence, is going Below the Line—a concept we explained in the first chapter of this section. It's a human reaction, natural and sometimes unavoidable. But while going Below the Line is natural, staying there is not.

In our corporate environment, we embrace a culture that acknowledges going Below the Line as part of our human experience. It's not about never slipping; it's about how quickly and effectively we can correct our course. During team calls, sometimes frustrations make us want to go Below the Line, and we are 100% okay with that. Knowing our human nature, we allow ourselves designated times to deliberately go Below the Line—venting, expressing frustration, or feeling disappointment, all within a controlled environment and usually with a sense of humor. After a few minutes of this, we switch gears: "Okay, let's move Above the Line now." It's a softer, more mindful approach to meeting management.

The next time you're on a team call, take note of how much time is spent Below the Line compared to above it. Consider the impact on productivity and morale. You might even ask the team, "I wonder if we're Below the Line right now. How can we move above it?" In this way, you are not placing blame for the tone of the conversation—you are simply helping lift others up.

Instead of assigning blame or letting these moments hinder our progress, we use them as catalysts for growth and insight. This brings us to the concept of the Accountability Gap. This gap is not about what is missing; it's about identifying where we currently are versus where we aim to be, and strategically addressing this disparity with the SHIFT mindset. The SHIFT mindset is the move from control to service:

Stop Fighting Reality: Acknowledge the current situation as it is, not as we wish it to be. Accepting reality forms the baseline from which genuine improvement can begin.

Have Faith: Trust in the capabilities and potential of the team to bridge the gap. You don't have all the answers, nor do you need to.

Identify What's Yours: Focus on how you contribute to the current state and what changes you can make to influence positive outcomes.

Free from Fear: Come from a place of willing the good of the other—the antidote to self-centered, fear-based thinking.

Take the Next Right Action: Determine and commit to practical steps that move us closer to our objectives. This involves clear, actionable strategies that individuals and teams can execute.

With the SHIFT mindset as our foundation, we move to practical application through the SOSD model—four critical questions that transform leaders from managers into coaches. This approach ensures that leaders do not bear undue burdens but instead empower their teams.

The Accountability Gap Framework

This framework helps leaders and teams not just manage but lead through accountability. It is based in the SOSD model shared in the previous chapter. Ask these four questions whenever someone is challenged with a gap in driving Key Results.

1. **See it**: Ask, "What is going on?" Or, put in other words, "What reality do we need to acknowledge?" Begin by coaching your colleague to recognize and define what needs improvement.

2. **Own it**: What about that can you control? Or put another way, what are you contributing to that gap? This step shifts focus from external obstacles to personal contribution and control.

3. **Solve it**: What else can you try? This involves creative problem-solving. And if you can't come up with anything, raise the stakes. Ask, if your life depended on it, what else could you do?

4. **Do it**: Set clear commitments. Once they've solved it, ask, "What will you do and by when?" This final question helps the person commit to actionable steps toward closing the gap.

When you see someone struggling or notice behaviors Below the Line, the approach isn't to point fingers but to guide a shift in perspective. "What would it look like for us to move Above the Line?" is a question that invokes a team's collective intelligence to rise above challenges. This not only fosters a culture of personal responsibility but also enhances team cohesion and support.

By nurturing an environment where accountability is understood as a shared and personal journey, we strengthen our organizational fabric. Every member feels empowered to identify gaps, own their part in them, creatively solve problems, and take decisive actions toward solutions. Through this, we not only achieve our Key Results more effectively, but we also create a workplace where accountability is a natural, integrated part of our culture.

For a quick reference on how to implement what you've learned in this chapter, visit surrendertolead.com/resources. There you will find our Accountability Gap Tool.

CHAPTER 21

INTERPRETING
EXPERIENCES

In late 1999, the world faced a crisis of confidence—not in politics but in computers. The looming Y2K bug, a programming oversight in which older computer systems stored dates using only the last two digits of the year, had sparked worldwide panic. Would computers crash when the clock struck midnight on January 1, 2000? Would planes fall from the sky? Would financial systems collapse?

Governments scrambled. Companies hired consultants. Uncertainty remained.

The Chinese government did something bold—something no memo, training program, or press release could replicate. They urged top executives of every major airline to be airborne in their planes at the stroke of midnight on January 1, 2000.[24] The message was simple: If you say it's safe, prove it.

There were no lengthy emails about confidence. No trust-building offsites. No motivational posters. Just one directive—fly. And they did. Executives boarded flights, passengers followed suit, and the stroke of midnight came and went without a single incident. The belief was driven instantly: The system is safe. Not because someone said so, but because the leaders were willing to bet their lives on it.

There are different types of experiences that you can create as a leader.

This is what we call a Type One experience—an experience so powerful, so direct, so unambiguous that it drives belief without interpretation. The belief wasn't explained. It was felt. It was lived. And it stuck.

For leaders, the lesson is clear: If you want to drive belief, create experiences that make interpretation unnecessary. Be willing to take the same leap you're asking your people to take. Put yourself on the plane.

But that's only one kind of experience—and most of us aren't ordering airline executives into the sky at midnight. In reality, most of the experiences leaders create are messier. More ambiguous. More easily misinterpreted. And if you want to take full accountability for your culture, you need to take full accountability for how your people interpret the experiences you create. Especially when the message isn't obvious.

Most leadership moments don't come with a runway and a headline. Most experiences happen in office hallways, Zoom calls, and Slack threads. They're more subtle, more frequent, and far more open to interpretation.

When a new CEO took the helm of a beauty retailer based outside Dallas, Texas, he noticed something strange right away. Everyone was at the office at least ten to fifteen minutes early— every single day. At first he figured it was just people trying to make a good impression. But it kept happening. Every meeting started on time. No one lingered in the halls. And when he tried to chat with people, no one would make eye contact. He couldn't get anyone to open up.

Eventually, he pulled aside someone who'd been with the company for twenty years and said, "You gotta help me. What is going on here?"

The longtime employee gave a polite chuckle and replied, "Well, your predecessor used to sit out front on Friday mornings. If anyone was late, he'd pink slip them on the spot."

"You're kidding."

"Not even a little. He'd fire people right there in the parking lot."

That explained everything. People weren't just being punctual—they were scared. The organization had internalized a belief that CEOs are not to be trusted. They are to be avoided. They wield power arbitrarily, and you better not get on their bad side.

The new CEO realized he had inherited not just a team but a deeply embedded belief system. So he decided to shake things up. The next Friday, he stood out front with a table of doughnuts, juice, and coffee—right in the same spot where his predecessor used to hand out terminations. As people arrived (still early, of course), he greeted them with, "Hi, welcome. It's good to have you on board."

The message landed. People were stunned. A few smiles. A few thank-yous. It was an early signal that things might be different.

But it didn't last. Doughnuts alone don't change beliefs. Especially when the belief is baked in by years of negative experiences. The CEO realized he had to keep going—keep creating experience after experience that told a new story.

He started every meeting by giving recognition to someone on the team. He made a point of asking for feedback and really listening to it. He showed up consistently, with openness and humility, and slowly, things began to shift. The beliefs changed, not because of one dramatic gesture but because the narrative people carried in their heads about leadership changed.

The doughnut table was a Type One experience. No interpretation required. It was obvious. It said: "I'm not the last guy." But the work after that? Those were Type Two experiences—meaningful but not self-explanatory. They needed framing. They needed consistency. They needed reinforcement.

That's what interpreting experiences is about. Taking responsibility not just for what happens but for what it means. Because when you don't, people fill in the blanks on their own. Think of it like this: You cancel a recurring team meeting without explanation. You know it's because your child is sick and you can't make it anymore, but what does your team think?

Maybe they assume you're too busy. Maybe they think the meeting didn't matter to begin with. Maybe they think you're unhappy with the team's performance and pulling away. Same action. Dozens of possible interpretations. Only one of them is the truth.

That's the danger. And it's avoidable—if you understand the four types of experiences and take accountability for how they land. Let's break them down.

- **Type One**: Clear, powerful, and unmissable. These experiences don't need interpretation because their meaning is obvious. The Y2K flight? Type One. The CEO handing out doughnuts in the same spot where his predecessor fired people? Also Type One. The belief is absorbed instantly— no translation needed.

- **Type Two**: Ambiguous but full of potential. These experiences could drive the right belief—but only if you help interpret them. Left alone, Type Two experiences are a coin toss. But with active interpretation? They can become transformational.
- **Type Three**: Neutral and forgettable. These are the everyday rhythms that don't shape belief in any meaningful way. Your weekly team sync. The fact that the coffee machine is always stocked. These experiences are background noise. They don't hurt you, but they don't help you either.
- **Type Four**: The dangerous ones. These are always misunderstood, always misinterpreted, and almost always create beliefs you don't want. These actions send loud, unintended messages—and once that belief is formed, it's hard to undo.

Most of leadership is navigating Types Two and Four. And that means you can't just create an experience and walk away. You have to own the interpretation. You have to name it, frame it, and reinforce it.

In February 2025, Chevron announced layoffs of about 9,000 people at the same time the oil producer planned a $66.5 million renovation of its headquarters in Houston.[25] It doesn't matter how much interpretation Chevron tried to share around this, it would always send a message that the leadership team likely does not want out in the world.

All of these examples show the same truth: People don't believe what you say; they believe what they experience. And if the experience isn't clear, they'll fill in the blanks themselves.

Usually with assumptions shaped by confirmation bias, belief bias, and their own past.

You can't eliminate those biases. But you can account for them. You can take responsibility not just for what people see, but for what they walk away believing. That's what interpreting experiences is all about. You have to own the interpretation. You have to name it, frame it, and reinforce it.

- **Name it**: Call out the experience as it happens. Don't let silence create stories. Say something like, "I'm canceling this meeting because my daughter is sick, and I can't give it my focused attention. Not because I'm disengaged."
- **Frame it**: Share the intention behind the action. Help people understand what you're really trying to communicate. "I trust you all to move forward without me today."
- **Reinforce it**: Back it up with consistent behavior. If you say you trust the team, then demonstrate it by continuing to empower them in the days and weeks that follow. Show alignment between what you say and what you do. That's how beliefs get locked in.

This framework is especially important for Type Two experiences, which live or die by how you frame them. But it's also your safety net for avoiding Type Four disasters.

In the next chapter, we'll talk about how to respond when difficult experiences have already shaped negative beliefs—how to rebuild trust and repair damage. But this chapter is about something even more powerful: prevention.

Interpreting experiences before they're misunderstood isn't just good communication—it's culture insurance. It's how you stay ahead of the narrative, protect trust before it breaks, and build a belief system that doesn't need repairing later.

Because once a story takes hold, it's hard to rewrite. But if you name it, frame it, and reinforce it from the start, you won't have to. Culture doesn't just happen to people. It happens through them. And the stories they tell themselves about what leadership means, what behavior is valued, and what the future holds—that's your culture, whether you like it or not.

CHAPTER 22

DIFFICULT EXPERIENCES

When we came together and Culture Partners acquired my (Jessica's) business, we both knew it wasn't going to be smooth sailing.

Joe was intentional about the hire. He believed in me. I believed in him. We both believed in the company and the intellectual property it was built on. And yet, within the organization, there was some inevitable change resistance. I was an outsider. I hadn't been hired by the founders. I hadn't spent years growing with the company. People wondered—out loud at times—why the role of chief strategy officer should go to someone from the outside.

We stepped into the partnership with eyes wide open, but I would be lying if I said it didn't get to me. I could feel the resistance in some meetings—not overt hostility but that quiet tension. The side glances. The flat reactions. The silence after I spoke.

A few months in, Joe and I put together our first big initiative—a research partnership with Stanford. I was proud of the work. It was ambitious. It was solid. It was also new to the way of doing things at Culture Partners.

I presented the plan to the team. Everyone listened quietly, but then, our chief product officer, Eric, raised his hand. He didn't raise his voice. He didn't even raise an eyebrow. But what followed was a barrage of questions:

- "How will this hold up across different verticals?"
- "What if Stanford doesn't align on timing?"
- "Is this methodology scalable?"
- "Have you considered what this means for our road map next quarter?"
- "And what about implementation risk?"

I nodded. I answered. I pivoted where I needed to. But when I walked out of that meeting, I wasn't thinking about my answers. I was thinking, *Eric is not on my team.*

Because here's the truth: I suffer from a common disease—one you probably suffer from too. It is the disease of MSU: Making Stuff Up.

We all do it. We make up stories in our heads to fill in the blanks. We create narratives about other people's motives, fears, power plays, alliances, and opinions. And most of the time? We're wrong. But we act like we're right. We let those stories run wild in our minds, shaping how we treat each other, how we show up, and what we believe.

In my mind, Eric was poking holes to undermine me. He didn't trust me. He didn't believe in me. He was testing me—and not in a collaborative, "iron sharpens iron" way. He was out to prove my plan didn't hold water.

And so, I reacted like many of us do when we MSU—I shut down. I didn't go to him. I didn't clarify. I didn't check my assumptions. I made stuff up, and then I walked away with a closed heart.

Most difficult experiences at work aren't born from malice—they're born from misunderstanding.

We operate in silos of perception. And when something rubs us the wrong way, we default to the most accessible explanation—usually one rooted in fear: *They don't respect me. They don't believe in me. They're out to get me.*

We don't just do this with our colleagues—we do this with our partners, our teams, our managers, our kids.

The reason MSU is so dangerous is because we start treating our made-up stories as truth. And then we act accordingly. We avoid the person. We gossip. We stew. We politely ice them out. We create experiences for them that reinforce the very beliefs we fear are true. It becomes a cycle. A cultural cancer.

It's not just personal—it's systemic. When leaders MSU, it shapes the organization. It creates beliefs that calcify into dysfunction. Resentments grow. Miscommunication festers. Trust erodes. And all because we're reacting to stories in our own heads instead of reality.

Harvard professor Chris Argyris mapped this behavior in a framework called the Ladder of Inference. Here's how it works:

1. **We observe an experience.** (Eric asked me lots of questions.)
2. **We select data.** (He only questioned *my* plan, not anyone else's.)
3. **We add meaning.** (He's trying to poke holes.)
4. **We make assumptions.** (He doesn't trust me.)
5. **We draw conclusions.** (He's not on my team.)

6. **We adopt beliefs.** (Eric is a roadblock.)
7. **We act on those beliefs.** (I avoid Eric and loop Joe in instead.)[26]

The higher up the ladder we climb, the further we get from reality. And the trickiest part? It happens fast. In seconds. The brain fills in the blanks before we've even had a chance to question the logic.

When we encounter tension at work, most of us default to one of five conflict styles: avoidance, accommodation, competition, compromise, or collaboration. Avoiders shut down. Accommodators give in. Competitors escalate. Compromisers meet halfway, even when the outcome isn't ideal. But collaborators—the rarest style—stay curious. They seek understanding, not victory.

We want to give you a framework that helps you move toward that collaborative style. It gives you language to explore conflict without accusation, helping both people feel seen and heard. And when you build that kind of culture, trust compounds fast.

So how do we stop MSU in its tracks?

We surrender to the idea that we don't know everything. That our assumptions might be wrong. That the stories in our heads are just that—stories. And we choose to create intentional experiences instead.

The Results Pyramid teaches us that experiences shape beliefs, which drive actions, which create results.

Here's the framework:

"The experience I had when you _____ led me to the belief that _____. Is that the belief you would like me to hold?"

It's simple. It's disarming. And it works.

Using this language shifts the conversation away from *you* language—which often feels like an attack—and reframes it through the lens of *it* language. "The experience I had when . . ." positions the issue as a third-party observation, rather than a personal accusation. It externalizes the conflict. You're not saying, "You were rude," or "You don't support me." You're simply describing the impact of an interaction and inviting the other person into a shared space of curiosity and understanding. That subtle shift creates psychological safety. It opens the door for dialogue rather than defensiveness, which is essential for intentional culture creation.

Psychological safety is what makes or breaks a culture's ability to grow. And nothing erodes that safety faster than *you* language. When someone hears, "You made me feel . . ." or "You don't support me," their brain registers a threat. Their defenses go up. Even if they don't react outwardly, internally they've shut down. But when you use experience-based language—when you talk about *how something landed* rather than what someone did—it lowers the temperature. It invites dialogue instead of defensiveness. That's what creates safety: not silence, not niceness, but the ability to have hard conversations without fear of judgment, retribution, or shame.

So, I applied the framework with Eric. I said: "The experience I had when you asked me all those questions during my presentation led me to the belief that you think my project is flawed and you don't believe it will be successful. Is that the belief you want me to hold?"

He looked surprised. And then he smiled.

"Oh no!" he said. "Jessica, I think your project is phenomenal. I'm detail-oriented, and I've done a lot of work like this before. My instinct is to stress-test a plan, to poke at it until I can help make it bulletproof. The belief I want you to hold is that I support you. I want this to be a home run. What experience do you need from me to hold that belief?"

We talked. Really talked. And that was the beginning of a shift.

One of the hardest parts about conflict is the silent conviction that *we are right*. That our view is the most reasonable, our solution the most logical, our way the best way. That's self-will. It's the quiet belief that if everyone just saw things how we see them, the team would run smoother, the project would go better, the results would come faster. And yet, that's exactly the trap. Self-will says: *My experience matters most.*

The antidote? Willing the good of another. True leadership isn't about getting your way—it's about creating space for others to feel safe, seen, and successful. When you choose to get curious instead of getting your way, you're surrendering your ego in service of something bigger. That is love. That is culture creation. That is how alignment happens. And that is taking accountability for results.

Eric didn't just help improve the research project—he became one of my closest thought partners. Today, he's the CTO of an AI company, and we still talk frequently about the future of AI at work. He's one of the smartest people I know.

All because I chose to replace MSU with truth. Because I surrendered the need to be "right" about his intentions and chose to be curious instead. This is how you move from fear to love. From misalignment to clarity. From tension to trust.

This is how you overcome difficult experiences without losing yourself in the story.

This is how you surrender to lead.

CONCLUSION

JUST DO IT

One of the most compelling stories of surrendering to the result, focusing on impact, and achieving unexpected success is the story of Nike and its cofounder Phil Knight—especially the company's legendary "Just Do It" marketing campaign.

Knight and his partner Bill Bowerman started out in the 1970s with a mission to try to make the perfect running shoe. But ten years later, they were simply trying to survive. Struggling against titans like Adidas, they fought tooth and nail to stay in the game. Sales were rocky. Resources were scarce. Doubt crept in. Knight even considered walking away.

Even after the breakout success of the Air Jordan shoe, worn by young basketball superstar Michael Jordan, Nike had entered the public consciousness but was still seen as just a running-shoe company that made a popular basketball shoe.

The real breakthrough came when they shifted their focus— not toward making the perfect shoe but toward understanding the impact their product could have on athletes. That shift in belief led to a new kind of innovation: not incremental but human-centered. They stopped obsessing over what the shoe was and started dreaming about what it could do for people.

Nike surrendered the need to be the best technically and instead focused on creating emotional resonance—something that could inspire greatness. "Just Do It" wasn't just a slogan. It was a belief system. A Cultural Belief rooted in surrendering the need for certainty and acting with courage anyway.

And it worked. Not because they micromanaged every step of the process but because they trusted their people, their story, and their why. They didn't just build a brand. They built a movement.

Again, let's be clear: Surrender is not passive. Surrender is not giving up, and it's certainly not a weapon to be wielded with judgment against others. The idea of "just do it" can be warped into a pressure-filled mantra that demands action at all costs. That's not what surrender is.

The shift to surrender means focusing on creating the conditions where the next right action reveals itself—through clarity, alignment, and accountability. Sometimes, though, you won't feel ready. The belief won't be there yet. The fear will still be loud. That's okay.

Because sometimes, you can't think your way into right acting; you have to act your way into right thinking.

Not fake it. Not hustle blindly. But take the next small, faithful step—*even when it's uncomfortable*. Especially when it's uncomfortable. Because movement itself creates clarity. Action, when rooted in love instead of fear, becomes the very thing that shifts belief.

With the framework in this book, you now have the road map. You understand the Results Equation:

Purpose + Strategy + Culture = Results

With this framework, proven by research and backed by real-world results, you can now surrender and focus on the process. You can stop trying to control everyone and everything and focus on what you can control, creating powerful experiences for those around you. You can lead from love, not ego. And when you do, you'll realize this truth: There is no middle ground. You're either leading from abundance or from scarcity, growing or dying. Living from love or operating from fear. Surrendering to scale or clinging to smallness.

The True Definition of Leadership

I (Joe) was on a call with Jim Snee, then the CEO of Hormel Foods, shortly after the COVID-19 pandemic began. About 1,200 people work at their worldwide headquarters in Austin, Minnesota, that includes corporate services, research and development, and a 12,500-square-foot Innovation Center with two kitchens and spaces for collaboration and training. This is not an environment made for remote work. Jim had a connection with many employees that came about through years of interaction in the office.

In our discussion, we talked about the pivot to remote work and the challenges Hormel Foods—and frankly all companies—were facing at the time: how to keep employees engaged, connected, and aligned in a world that had suddenly become virtual. All without the rhythms, rituals, and in-person interactions that once held teams together.

Jim is as steady and loyal as they come, so it's no surprise that the sudden shift to remote work felt disorienting—even for him. It wasn't that he lacked trust in his people—that was never in question. But everything had changed overnight, and the familiar playbook no longer applied. Naturally, our conversation wound back to culture—the culture of clarity, alignment, and accountability that he helped build. He recognized that he didn't need to have every answer. What he needed was conviction in what he knew to be true—that his team was capable, that the culture was strong, and that caring for people mattered more than ever. Jim led the organization with empathy and steadiness. And in a time of deep uncertainty, he anchored the company by trusting the Cultural Beliefs that made it strong in the first place. That's how great leaders show up when it matters most.

If you take nothing else from this book, remember this: Leadership is the ability to set the conditions for success. That requires the humility to accept what you can't control, the courage to change what you can, and the wisdom to know the difference. This is where surrender comes in. Leadership is not about control—it's about surrendering what was never yours to begin with. You can't control other people—their reactions, resistance, pace, preferences, or performance.

But you can control yourself—your presence, your integrity, your mindset. And even more than that, you can control the experiences you create for others. That's the job of a leader—not to control outcomes but to surrender the illusion of control and focus instead on shaping the conditions where the best outcomes become possible.

And setting the conditions means creating experiences.

First, create **Clarity** through the Results Equation. When you're clear on purpose, strategy, and culture, you create a shared lens through which everyone can see the goal and their role in reaching it.

Then, drive **Alignment** by designing experiences that reinforce that clarity. Recognition systems, storytelling, feedback loops—everything that signals "this is who we are, and this is how we win."

And finally, take **Accountability** for how you show up every day. Not to police performance, but to drive alignment through empowerment. Because here's the truth: Too many people are waiting to be empowered. As if empowerment is something you receive, like a promotion or a permission slip. It's not. Empowerment is something you take. It's something you do.

As a leader, your job is to model that. To show that you're not waiting for someone else to lead better, show up differently, or care more. You're starting with yourself. You're shifting the story. You're embodying the change.

The SHIFT begins with you.

Clarity, alignment, and accountability—lived by you first—create a culture where everyone else can rise too. You now understand how to connect purpose with strategy and activate that with culture, to deliver the results you need in any situation. Whether it is an individual, a team, a department, or a company of hundreds of thousands of employees. The equation is limitless in its scale.

You now have a step-by-step system for creating the road map specific to your unique situation to deliver the results you want. The Results Equation works. The SHIFT works. And surrender isn't just a spiritual concept—it's a business strategy.

You're here to create the conditions where greatness can unfold. We've shown you the stories. We've given you the tools. We've given you the data. Now comes the hard part: Just do it.

ACKNOWLEDGMENTS

At Culture Partners, we are deeply grateful to the people who make our work meaningful. To our colleagues—thank you for your commitment, your care, and your belief in what culture can do. You live this work every day.

A heartfelt thank you to Paul Sloan for helping us bring clarity to complex ideas and challenging us to think more deeply and courageously. And to Mattson Newell, whose partnership and perspective were essential in pulling this all together—thank you.

We also want to honor the founders of Culture Partners, Tom Smith and Roger Connors, who created powerful models and frameworks that continue to shape our work today. Thank you for your vision and for passing the torch.

To our readers, Andrew Collier, Lynn Smith, and the many brilliant people we work with—thank you for your insight, collaboration, and encouragement.

And most importantly, to our clients: thank you for your trust, your openness, and your shared commitment to change. You are helping us fulfill our vision of impacting five million lives. We are honored to be on this journey with you.

NOTES

Chapter 1

1   "Cristiano Ronaldo: 'I'm the Most Complete Player to Have Existed,'"
    FOX Sports, February 4, 2025, https://www.foxsports.com/stories/
    soccer/cristiano-ronaldo-im-most-complete-player-have-existed.

2   "Lionel Messi: 'What Motivates Me Is . . .'" Football Espana,
    December 3, 2018, https://www.football-espana.net/2018/12/03/
    lionel-messi-what-motivates-me-is.

3   The Results Pyramid was first introduced in a book by the founders of
    Culture Partners. Roger Connors, Tom Smith, and Craig Hickman, *The
    Oz Principle: Getting Results Through Individual and Organizational
    Accountability* (Prentice Hall, 1994).

Chapter 2

4   Patty McCord, "How Netflix Reinvented HR," *Harvard Business
    Review*, January-February 2014, https://hbr.org/2014/01/
    how-netflix-reinvented-hr.

5   *The Josh Bersin Company Podcast*, "Why Does Netflix Outperform? They
    Are a 'Dynamic Organization.' Here's What We've Learned," joshbersin.
    com, January 27, 2024, https://joshbersin.com/podcast/why-does-
    netflix-outperform-they-are-a-dynamic-organization-heres-what-
    weve-learned.

Chapter 4

6   Barb Darrow, "Oracle Cloud Chief Shawn Price Dies at 53,"
     Fortune, October 26, 2016, https://fortune.com/2016/10/26/
     oracle-exec-shawn-price-dies/.

7   Oracle, "2025 Third Quarter Financials," Investor.oracle.com, March 10,
     2025, https://investor.oracle.com/financials/default.aspx.

Chapter 5

8   Naina Dhingra and Bill Schaninger, "How to Unleash the Power of
     Purpose at Work and in Life," McKinsey.com, June 3, 2021, https://www.
     mckinsey.com/capabilities/people-and-organizational-performance/
     our-insights/the-search-for-purpose-at-work.

9   Jordan Turner, "Employees Increasingly Seek Value and Purpose at
     Work," Gartner.com, March 29, 2023, https://www.gartner.com/en/
     articles/employees-seek-personal-value-and-purpose-at-work-be-
     prepared-to-deliver.

10   DDI, "Global Leadership Forecast 2018," DDIworld.com, 2018, https://
     www.ddiworld.com/research/global-leadership-forecast-2018.

11   Ryan Landau, "HBR Says This Is How You Turn Purpose into
     Performance," Purpose.jobs, August 23, 2018, https://www.
     purpose.jobs/blog/hbr-says-this-is-how-you-turn-purpose-into-
     performance#:~:text=%E2%80%9CYou%20do%20not%20invent%20
     a,is%20a%20disciplined%2C%20iterative%20process.

12   Harvard Business Review Analytic Services, "The Business Case for
     Purpose," *Harvard Business Review*, April 20, 2016, https://hbr.org/
     resources/pdfs/comm/ey/19392HBRReportEY.pdf.

Chapter 7

13   E. A. Locke and G. P. Latham, "Building a Practically Useful Theory
     of Goal Setting and Task Motivation: A 35-Year Odyssey," *American
     Psychological Association* 57, no. 9 (2002): 705–717, https://psycnet.apa.
     org/doiLanding?doi=10.1037%2F0003-066X.57.9.705.

14   George A. Miller, "The Magical Number Seven, Plus or Minus Two:
     Some Limits on Our Capacity for Processing Information," *Psychological
     Review* 63, no. 2 (1956): 81–97. https://labs.la.utexas.edu/gilden/
     files/2016/04/MagicNumberSeven-Miller1956.pdf.

15   "What Is the Mysterious Rule of Three?" Rule-of-three.co.uk, October 22, 2021, https://www.rule-of-three.co.uk/articles/what-is-the-rule-of-three-copywriting.

Chapter 8

16   Alex Camp, Arne Gast, Drew Goldstein, and Brooke Weddle, "Organizational Health Is (Still) the Key to Long-Term Performance," McKinsey.com, February 12, 2024, https://www.mckinsey.com/capabilities/people-and-organizational-performance/our-insights/organizational-health-is-still-the-key-to-long-term-performance.

Chapter 10

17   Andy Jassy, "Update from Amazon CEO Andy Jassy on Return-to-Office Plans and Manager Team Ratio," Aboutamazon.com, September 16, 2024, https://www.aboutamazon.com/news/company-news/ceo-andy-jassy-latest-update-on-amazon-return-to-office-manager-team-ratio.

Chapter 13

18   Carol S. Dweck, *Mindset: The New Psychology of Success* (Random House, 2006).

19   "Doug Merritt | Aviatrix." Aviatrix.com. February 5, 2025, https://aviatrix.com/leader/doug-merritt/.

Chapter 15

20   "Ownership Works & Ingersoll Rand Case Study," YouTube, April 4, 2022, https://youtu.be/qcEuw8GKfO4.

21   Jessica Kriegel, "KKR's Pete Stavros on Shared Ownership and CEO Empathy," YouTube, March 18, 2025, https://www.youtube.com/watch?v=IAsrzW-uuNc.

Chapter 18

22   Gary Can, "The Development of the Book of Worship for United States Forces A," Duke University divinity school thesis, April 25, 1996, https://apps.dtic.mil/sti/pdfs/ADA313938.pdf.

Chapter 19

23   *Culture Leaders: The Masters Behind the Movements* podcast, "Leading with Integrity: Scott Wine on Faith, Discipline, and Transforming Company Culture," YouTube, October 28, 2024, https://www.youtube.com/watch?v=QzUkR1HC2QI.

Chapter 21

24   Christopher Reynolds, "Airlines' Y2K Readiness: Blue Skies or Turbulence?" *Los Angeles Times*, August 8, 1999, https://www.latimes.com/archives/la-xpm-1999-aug-08-tr-63622-story.html.

25   Priyansha Mistry, "Chevron Layoffs Push More Employees Out of Work in 2025," *The HR Digest*, February 13, 2025, https://www.thehrdigest.com/chevron-layoffs-push-more-employees-out-of-work-in-2025/.

Chapter 22

26   Chris Argyris, *Overcoming Organizational Defenses: Facilitating Organizational Learning* (Allyn & Bacon, 1990).

ABOUT THE AUTHORS

Jessica Kriegel is a workplace culture expert, keynote speaker, and researcher. As chief strategy officer at Culture Partners, she leads research and thought leadership that challenges traditional ideas about control, power, and performance, offering bold new approaches that get results. A seasoned, dynamic speaker and host of the *CEO Daily Brief* and *Culture Leaders* podcasts, she is a frequent guest on CNN, Fox Business, CNBC, and Bloomberg. Jessica holds an MBA and a doctorate in educational leadership, and is currently pursuing a Master of Divinity. She is also a trained death doula, a role that deepens her approach to leading with presence and care. Her first book, *Unfairly Labeled*, challenges assumptions about generational stereotypes in the workplace.

Joe Terry is the CEO of Culture Partners, the leader in delivering results-driven culture transformation. For the past forty years, Joe has dedicated his life to the study and practice of optimizing human potential in sport, life, and business. As a five-time chief executive, he has successfully built, led, and grown organizations focused on serving employees, customers, and communities. In

2018 he was inducted into the HKW (Private Equity) Hall of Fame for demonstrating exceptional leadership, talent, integrity, and remarkable shareholder return. Joe is also a highly accomplished athlete, having played linebacker in the NFL and competed in fifteen (and counting) Ironman races, including three times at the Ironman World Championships in Kona, Hawaii.